SHAKE-OUT

SHAKE-OUT

Iowa Farm Families in the 1980s

MARK FRIEDBERGER

THE UNIVERSITY PRESS OF KENTUCKY

Copyright © 1989 by The University Press of Kentucky

Scholarly publisher for the Commonwealth,
serving Bellarmine College, Berea College, Centre
College of Kentucky, Eastern Kentucky University,
The Filson Club, Georgetown College, Kentucky
Historical Society, Kentucky State University,
Morehead State University, Murray State University,
Northern Kentucky University, Transylvania University,
University of Kentucky, University of Louisville,
and Western Kentucky University.

Editorial and Sales Offices: Lexington, Kentucky 40506-0336

Library of Congress Cataloging-in-Publication Data
Friedberger, Mark.
    Shake-out : Iowa farm families in the 1980s / Mark Friedberger.
        p.   cm.
    Includes bibliographical references.
    ISBN 0-8131-1682-1 (alk. paper)
        1. Farmers—Iowa—Economic conditions. 2. Rural families—Iowa—
    Economic conditions. 3. Agriculture—Economic aspects—Iowa.
    I. Title.
    HD8039.F32U645   1989
    338.1'09777'09048—dc20   89-36474
                                                                   CIP

This book is printed on acid-free paper meeting
the requirements of the American National Standard
for Permanence of Paper for Printed Library Materials.
                              ∞

To
MJF and EF
and to the memory of ELF

Contents

Tables

Preface

This book really began on a hot and humid summer day in 1981 as I drove north through the Iowa countryside. Land was selling in some areas for over three thousand dollars an acre; farm foreclosures had been largely unknown since the Great Depression; the biggest economic worry of farm families was how to pay the inheritance taxes on the back forty. I knew that the severe inflation and the cost-price squeeze of the late seventies and early eighties had affected farm families, but my primary interest that morning was to begin a historical research project based on the musty old records to be found in the basements and attics of courthouses. As was the case with many other observers of rural America, the farm crisis caught me unawares.

By 1983 I had collected most of the material I needed in Iowa and had decided to attempt a similar project in the California Central Valley. I spent much of 1984 in the West, doing the necessary research for a historical comparison of family farming in California and Iowa. Quite by chance I picked up an Iowa newspaper around Christmas of 1984 and read about the worsening economic situation. It was obvious that the situation unfolding in many Iowa communities had some historical precedent, and I realized that I could not ignore the contemporary scene in any discussion of long-term change. Thus, it was with a description of the sharp downturn of the eighties that I concluded my history of agriculture and family farming in Iowa and California in the twentieth century.[1]

I began to study the Iowa farm crisis in more detail in 1985, and from then until the summer of 1987 I lived in the state. This book is the result of that extended stay. It is avowedly interdisciplinary in scope, using a blend of history, rural sociology, journalism, politics, and field research to explore how a rural society underwent rapid change in the late twentieth century. I have approached this subject from the point of view of behavioral history, which, for the last twenty years, has broadened our understanding of the past by concentrating on the daily lives of ordinary people. Rather than recount the story of presidents, wars, and politicians, social historians have looked at society from "the bottom up," as I do here.

To a considerable extent this book builds on the research for *Farm Families and Change in Twentieth-Century America.* I use documentary evidence, the press, and participant observation to paint a picture of behavior at the grass roots, among farm families. In addition, I have also used interviews for systematic data collection.

In the main, I emphasize how farm families themselves reacted to the boom-and-bust environment of the late seventies and early eighties. To be sure, the involvement of activist organizations, the performance of the lending and legal professions, the parts played by the media and the farm programs cannot be ignored. Indeed, all these aspects of the crisis merit in-depth studies of their own. Here, however, they are scrutinized solely for their influence and impact on farmers and their families.[2]

It is important to point out that although I have borrowed many concepts from the social sciences, I have stopped short of the policy recommendations and analysis typical of social science. A social scientist usually studies a problem in order to build up theoretical knowledge so that society can attempt to solve it. For instance, a researcher studying farm family psychological stress during the farm crisis would begin with theoretical assumptions, test those assumptions, and then make recommendations not only for future study but also for improving services to families in need.[3] Historians, on the other hand, generally have no utilitarian motives in their work. They cast a critical eye over past events to formulate a thesis that can reasonably explain change. Their purpose is essentially to tell what happened.

In this instance a historian is, for all intents and purposes, documenting current events. For someone trained to conduct research in archives filled with old documents, this was role reversal with a vengeance. The writing of contemporary history can be a perilous business. Inevitably the passage of time tends to alter perspectives; events take on a different meaning in retrospect, no matter how well contemporary chroniclers do their work. The Iowa farm crisis is no exception. Hindsight reveals that what seemed to be a collapse of the state's economy in the winter of 1984-1985 was in fact a steep recession. Similarly, although the farm economy seemed to have finally recovered itself by early 1988, a severe drought in the corn belt in the spring and summer kindled fresh fears of further economic disruption.

To take this point a shade farther, a common topic of discussion among farmers in 1986 was whether the rural downturn was a precursor for a collapse of the national economy. The stock market crash of October 1987 suggested that such a prognosis was in the realm of possibility and that the history of the twenties and the thirties was about to repeat itself. Nevertheless, despite considerable uncertainty, no immediate calamity occurred. On the other hand, one parallel did suggest itself between the stock market crash and the bursting of the land bubble in Iowa: in all probability the investing public would be more cautious in the future. For like farmers who had leveraged themselves to buy land before the rural downturn, investors would respond to the shock of the loss of paper assets on the stock market with more conservative behavior.

But whatever the economic future in the final decade of the century, rapid structural change and uncertainty would seem to be the order of business in the nation as a whole. The Iowa farm crisis and the farm families who experienced its full impact, while inherently interesting in themselves, also provide a case study in how one segment of society reorients its priorities in a period of painful readjustment. The farm crisis forced agriculture to live within its means. It is possible that farm families were pioneers in learning to face, with lowered expectations, a future of declining living standards and limited business growth. More and more Americans may have to learn the same hard lesson in the next decade.

This study could not have been completed without grant 5 R01 AG04503 from the National Institute on Aging. Once again I would like to thank the institute for generous support over the period of research. In Iowa a number of individuals and institutions were most helpful with their time and facilities. The Coop-

erative Extension Service staff in Sac and Ida counties, Fran
Philips at the Rural Concern hotline in Des Moines, Joan Blundall at the Northwest Iowa Mental Health Center in Spencer, the
staffs in the recorders' offices in Fayette, Benton, Sac, and Ida
counties, the staffs of the Northern and Southern District of Iowa
bankruptcy courts in Cedar Rapids and Des Moines, Don Muhm,
farm editor at the Des Moines *Register*, and the staff at Prairiefire
in Des Moines—all smoothed the way for me.

I thank Peter McLennon, who time and time again went
beyond the bounds of friendship to provide facilities and en-
couragement when I returned to Chicago from Iowa. The final
version of this book would not have been written without his
help.

Last, I owe an enormous debt of gratitude to the anonymous
farm families described in these pages. They made this research
project a stimulating and at times exciting endeavor, an experience I will always cherish.

Introduction:
Iowa's Rural Heritage

"Iowa," one of her most discerning observers once said, "combines the qualities of half a dozen states, and perhaps that is the reason why it often seems the most undistinguished place in the world."[1] Such a statement, though it would surely touch a sensitive nerve in most Iowans, delineates an appealing characteristic for anyone attempting to draw inferences about the farm crisis from one state, indeed, from several small communities within that state.

This lack of distinctiveness can be traced to the settlement of Iowa, when an artificial organizational system was superimposed on the virgin prairie. Following the system designed by Thomas Jefferson, hundreds of centrally placed towns were laid out as service centers to the farm population who settled the surrounding countryside in the nineteenth century. A rigid grid of counties, townships, and sections crisscrossed the state, and thousands of dirt roads acted as section boundaries and rights of way. When the railroads came, such was their institutional power that they were permitted to cut diagonally across the landscape instead of following the grid system. Then, after about a century of service, many miles of track were torn up, and the railroad bed was returned to farmland. Partly to compensate, the state and counties built an extensive system of farm-to-market blacktop roads on the original dirt and gravel surfaces. In some areas of Iowa it is possible to drive for over a hundred miles without passing a settlement of more than a few hundred souls. Except for the elimination of fencerows to make larger fields and the abandonment of thousands of homesteads since World War II, the look of the land has not changed appreciably. Iowa has retained its rural character.

The Jeffersonian legacy so important in the layout of the state also has a bearing on many other aspects of Iowa life. Jefferson's system was meant in part to create a sense of community among a geographically dispersed population, which might otherwise have remained socially and politically isolated. In recent years this community interest has been maintained through a widespread interest in collegiate athletics, but community building at a statewide level has a much longer history. Newspapers and to some extent radio stations, wishing to appeal to as wide an audience as possible in a state with few metropolitan areas, have long emphasized statewide rather than local concerns. The Des Moines *Register*, for example, has attempted to attract an Iowa-wide audience from early in the twentieth century.

This newspaper was among the first in the nation to sponsor a statewide public opinion poll, appropriately so, for George Gallup was born in Iowa. By its very name the Iowa Poll indicated that Iowans had a collective mentality that could be quantified. Moreover, the idea was built on the Jeffersonian notion that in a democratic republic the ideas of ordinary folk matter. Iowa, as the classic manifestation of the Jeffersonian society peopled by yeoman farmers and small-town dwellers, deserved to have her population kept abreast of all relevant political, social, and economic information. Iowans came to expect the regular publication of data not usually made public in other states. Until the Great Depression, Iowa had the most comprehensive of all state censuses, and the state continues to make voluminous amounts of information available to this day. Lists of the salaries of state employees, including professors employed at state universities, and of recipients of large sums of money from federal farm programs, as well as the annual accounting of state banks, are some of the items that regularly appear in the press. As an assiduous community builder, the Des Moines *Register* also attempts to provide its readers with detailed information on anything or anybody that has a connection to the state. This "Iowa connection" syndrome portrays Iowa as a small community writ large, where anybody can know everything about anyone else.

For a dispersed population radio is a natural vehicle for community building. From the first, powerful commercial stations, together with those run by the state universities, have used the airwaves as a means of mass education. This tradition remains strong. In a world where for years AM radio has suffered the vagaries of the program director's desire to improve ratings, the two large public radio stations broadcast a veritable cornucopia of programming into the farthest reaches of the state and beyond. The BBC World Service news, all-night classical music, gavel-to-gavel coverage of the state legislature, hourly market reports, and daily readings of classic and popular books, are just some of the fare provided. The quality of the programming eases long drives between population centers and demonstrates the state's commitment to keep its citizens well informed.

The Jeffersonian legacy has had concrete implications for Iowa in the late twentieth century. Her population, unusually articulate and well informed on issues that affect them, has been quick to reject those who transgressed. The failure of incumbent United States senators to win reelection in the late seventies and early eighties was a case in point. But nowhere was the Jeffersonian legacy better memorialized than in the introduction of the Iowa caucuses, whose strategic timing ensured that presidential candidates had to spend an inordinate amount of time wooing Iowa voters. In a big urban state it was possible to meet intimately with politicians who were running for president only at functions where contributors paid a thousand dollars for the privilege; in small-town Iowa the early caucuses made it possible to meet all the candidates and discuss the issues one-on-one for the cost of a hamburger and coffee at the local cafe.[2] Not surprisingly, aggressive advocacy for farm issues was likely to win supporters, and "fighting for family farms" developed into a powerful issue.

For agriculture is the heart of Iowa, where rich prairie soil has allowed the state to become the world's leading producer of corn and hogs. The centrality of farming to the state's economy has been both an advantage and disadvantage. Farming has brought relative prosperity to Iowans, but specialization in agriculture has also made Iowa vulnerable to rapid economic change. The whole population has depended to some extent on agriculture for a livelihood, and this lack of diversification has proved especially risky for the rural communities where the families in this book live and work.

In small communities the farm crisis was yet another phase

in the unending battle against economic decline in the twentieth
century. As always, the weapon for fighting this decline was
boosterism. In the nineteenth century, communities vied to become the county seat, to be on a rail route, and if they were
fortunate, to host a state institution or college. In the late twentieth century small communities turned their attention to attracting industry. A well-educated and reliable work force that
would toil for a minimum wage, generous tax advantages, good
schools, and a clean, wholesome environment were the chief
selling points used to interest outsiders in establishing a plant.
But hundreds of small towns were able to offer similar incentives
to businesses, and the competition was intense.

Boosterism also had a natural affiliation with schools, for the
death warrant for many small towns was the closing of the local
school. School consolidations had a long history in Iowa, and
their divisiveness was legendary.[3] By the 1950s all rural one-
room schools had been consolidated. Communities continued to
decline, and many towns were threatened by the specter of
further consolidations. In some areas one school served the
whole county, and there was a distinct possibility that this
pattern would become more widespread. The importance of the
school for the small community cannot be exaggerated. It is often
the largest employer, and its sports teams and band are a rallying
point against decline, a focus of community identity.

Over the years, migration and intermarriage brought the
small-town and country populations closer together. The old
animosities that had marked relations between farm and town in
earlier decades disappeared.[4] The farm prosperity of the seventies stemmed the tide of decline in some communities. Small
towns, especially those within commuting distance of metropolitan areas, began to attract families employed in the city but
wanting to have the advantages of small-town living. In every
community, except those that had already lost hope, housing
stock was rehabilitated and retailing upgraded. Agribusinessmen, in particular, were never so prosperous.

Response to Change

The 1980s was a time of massive restructuring in the American
economy.[5] In the "rust belt" and in the rural heartland certain

industries, agriculture among them, were in the vanguard of this painful process. During the inflationary seventies many farmers had lived on borrowed money. The ever-rising equity value of their land allowed some to expand and modernize their operations. When in the early eighties inflation was controlled, the economic rules by which they had lived underwent a sudden reversal. No longer was an operation judged by the worth of its land, buildings, and equipment, but by the cash it could produce from its crops and livestock. This sudden shifting of gears was especially difficult to survive in an industry where adjustments must conform to a calendar of the seasons rather than rapid market changes. Corn-belt farmers deal not with assembly-line production but with growing plants and animals. They usually need eighteen months' lead time to adapt to a new economic climate. Unfortunately their lenders, who were the most visible orchestrators of adjustment, were not prepared to wait. The lender-farmer confrontation developed into one of the major themes of the Iowa farm crisis

As in any period of prolonged economic stress and confusion, change was resisted. The two principal antagonists, farmers and lenders, acted under the assumption that the economy would right itself in a year or so, refusing to face the realization that it would never be the same again. Change brought farmers and lenders face to face with the unknown. Some lenders were too rigid to negotiate with borrowers, and such behavior eventually led to the bankruptcy of the leading farm credit institution, the Farm Credit System.[6] Before the farm crisis farmers for the most part had docilely followed the recommendations of lenders, professionals, and experts, believing that they knew best. When the farm crisis demonstrated that the experts were so terribly wrong in their predictions about expansion, they suffered a severe loss of credibility. The initial trust of farmers for their bankers quickly dissipated once lenders began trying to recoup their losses through the accelerated, often ruthless collection of loans. Farmers fought back, and there followed a period of confrontation in which both sides resisted the inevitable changes in their way of doing business.

From the farmer's viewpoint, gone were the days when his financial position was settled over a yearly chat and handshake with the lender. The introduction of a more businesslike approach to financial planning and more efficient record keeping by computers drew resentment—a resentment fanned by the perception that lenders themselves were partly responsible for the difficulties of the farm family. Farmers tended to perceive the sudden change in business practices as both unwarranted and insulting. Lenders, for their part, blamed farmers for their lack of professionalism and resented their refusal to cut back on their standard of living once the boom was over.

These attitudes, and the distrust they generated, tended to persist. The passage in the spring of 1986 of state legislation mandating mediation between lender and farmer before a foreclosure could take place tended to force movement toward accepting change in economic relationships and to adjust operations and expectations. But misconceptions still abounded. The Farm Credit System showed its contempt for the process by throwing over a thousand cases into mediation in the first month of operation, swamping the new service. Farmers, in their turn, often made little effort to prepare for mediation. On both sides intransigence tended to make a mockery of the first steps toward the resolution of differences.

Another important theme of the farm crisis involved media attention. Extensive television coverage brought the poignancy of the downturn into every urban living room. Not surprisingly, television emphasized the dramatic rather than the mundane, stressed the emotional pain of leaving the farm that had been in the family for a century instead of the arcane rules and regulations that forced the hand of a lender under pressure from federal regulators. Moreover, in the late seventies and early eighties doom and gloom were the standard approach to farm stories on the networks. Time and again audiences saw farmers portraying themselves as victims. Whether the enemy was low prices or the intervention of nature, they were always "barely hanging on" or "just about to go under." This litany of woes was broadcast in good times as well as bad.[7] There was a danger that farmers could cry wolf once too often, and in the bad times ahead the public would ignore them. Why should the public be any more sympathetic to the plight of farmers than to that of steel workers? Both after all were being forced to adjust to structural changes in their industries. Repeated complaints might bring only an indifferent shrug, in the words of one farm wife worried about this sort of publicity, "Oh the farmers are crying again."[8]

In actual fact polls showed that some segments of the urban population were supportive of the movement to "save family farms." They were usually better educated and often had ties to the countryside through birth or relatives.[9] Such people were responsive to television messages about the plight of rural America, and farm activists did all they could to make sure that the message would be delivered. Their work constituted a third theme in the Iowa farm crisis.

Activist leadership played a key role in maximizing attention to the farm crisis, in ensuring that the public, the politicians, and the state and federal government paid heed to the farm problem. Symbolism had an important place in this effort to gain support, with cross plantings and other types of demonstrations aimed to influence both the media and the authorities. At the state level grass-roots activism was very effective in the years 1983-1985 and alerted Iowans to the possibility of a major economic breakdown. So successful were the activists that by the spring of 1985 state government had begun to mobilize its resources on behalf of farmers.[10]

Mainstream farm organizations such as the Farm Bureau were placed on the defensive in the early stages of the farm crisis, whereas the new grass-roots farmer-oriented organizations such as the Iowa Farm Unity Coalition gained credibility. From the very beginning they emphasized service to their clients, most visibly in their hotlines and their vigorous pursuit of farmers' rights.[11] Yet despite their early success, these upstarts did not achieve a universal following among the farm population as a whole over the long term.

The new organizations were unable to supplant their chief rival, the Farm Bureau, partly because the bureau had a long history and grass-roots membership in every township in the state. Moreover, the Farm Bureau's most important function was not farm organizing but the sale of insurance and other services. Again, the Iowa Farm Unity Coalition was perceived as radical by farmers who were generally politically conservative. In addition, their vision was somewhat distorted by their mission, for the majority of their contacts were with farm families who were struggling. So successful were the farm advocates in orienting the state toward mobilization to meet the crisis that the issue of saving the family farm became a sacred cow. By the summer of 1985 conservative Republicans, scrambling to place themselves on the right side of the issue, had begun acting like populists. Just before the 1986 elections the Republican governor, Terry Branstad, sued the Farm Credit System to halt foreclosure of farm properties. Two years before, he had been a firm advocate of Ronald Reagan's farm policies, whose cornerstone was a market free of government interference. Ironically, the effort to save family farms became so overwhelming that it had the effect of turning the Iowa farm crisis into something of a pseudocrisis.

The perception that the problems of agriculture were caused by shortcomings at the national rather than the state level brought another approach into play. Many believed that their salvation lay with the federal farm program as it was constituted. They began to pursue changes in that system.

Before the downturn, mainstream farm groups mouthed platitudes about the importance of free-market agriculture. Nevertheless, for all the rhetoric, farming was a "sheltered" sector of the economy. Because of its unique position, agriculture had always had a favored political and economic status. The tax and antitrust laws, for example, gave farmers certain exemptions in routine business dealings. Even more vital for survival were the ubiquitous farm subsidies begun in the 1930s, which had since virtually become entitlement programs. They played a part in deadening the sharp blows farm families received in the farm crisis. Milk subsidies, deficiency payments, nonrecourse loans, payment-in-kind certificates, and price supports were some of the benefits farm families could use to weather the sea change in the economy.

Despite the intention of the Reagan administration to jettison federal farm programs, their cost to the taxpayer grew dramatically, reaching $25.8 billion in 1986. In Iowa the farm crisis would probably have come earlier had not the government spent almost a billion dollars on the payment-in-kind program in 1983. This largesse kept some farmers solvent for another twelve months, but the removal of thousands of acres from production was a setback to the agribusiness community. Elevators, seed, and machinery dealers all suffered, and some never recovered. Many had to close their doors over the next few years. The mountain of grain stored in every conceivable type of facility by December 1986 was a testament to the ability of the farm lobby not only to persuade politicians to continue to support the feed grain program at high levels but also to permit the planting of millions of acres of corn and soybeans when world prices were low. The introduction of "market clearing" prices moved grain only gradually and had little effect on raising prices. On the other hand, the farm program did benefit both the grain trade (from storage fees) and farm families, who were able to pay off debt.

The promotion of an alternative to the costly farm program of 1985 by neopopulist farm advocates, received little favorable response from farmers. The Save the Family Farm Act revolved round the old mandatory controls of the New Deal. If a majority of the farmers who planted a particular crop agreed, the government would determine how much was needed to fill demand and what would be a fair price. Officials would then impose acreage allotments and marketing quotas on every farmer producing the crop to conform to those targets.[12]

Farmers were unwilling to try out the idea, even though it had some merit, and their response was another indicator of the fear of change in the farm community. (Ironically, the drought of 1988 seemed to justify this lack of innovative spirit.) Farmers saw mandatory controls as a conspiracy against freedom of choice, ignoring the fact that the 1985 program had turned them into welfare recipients in everything but name. Throughout the winter of 1986-1987 farmers spent hours waiting for appointments at the Agricultural Stabilization and Conservation Service, where their individual programs had to be approved. Farm journals openly gave advice on beating the fifty-thousand-dollar limit imposed by the United States Department of Agriculture.[13] Despite the threat of audits, hours of extra paper work, and the possibility that unsubstantiated payments would have to be returned, however, the majority of farmers preferred a farm program that was a known quantity. For the neopopulists, whose goals for farm families and farming went far beyond a scramble for government dollars, this expediency on the part of farmers was a disappointment. On the other hand, as will be shown, the neopopulist tenacity in pursuing the debt problem on behalf of farmers paid dividends when the federal Farm Credit System was restructured at the end of 1987.

Finally, although it took many months for the true nature of the crisis to show itself, one of the most important characteristics of the downturn was its selectivity in choosing victims. Unlike the Great Depression, the farm crisis caused hardship only to certain farm families. Most did not get into financial difficulties. Moreover, it is important to remember that farmers displayed their independence in regard to the assistance eventually mobilized on their behalf. A whole arsenal of programs aimed at alleviating the readjustment process after a farm failure—food stamps, legal assistance, psychological counseling, job retraining, to name just a few—demonstrated the great efforts made to bring the standard urban response to familial difficulties to the countryside. However, farmers showed that they would remain strongly independent in dealing with reorganization and adjustment. Farm activists fought long and hard to secure the rights of farmers in financial difficulties. State government mobilized to offer telephone counseling and farmer-creditor mediation as part of the official response to the crisis. But despite the intervention of well-intentioned outsiders, farm families often proved unresponsive to these initiatives. They preferred to work out their problems by themselves.[14]

Studying Farm Families

Farm families are both simple and fairly difficult to study. Information about them is readily available in the public records which provide information on land holdings, mortgages, probate, civil litigation, as well as demographic data. These can be combined with plat maps, which show where farmers live and own land. At the same time, while there is much information available in the public record, archives are dispersed over a wide area. There are ninety-nine counties in Iowa, each divided into as many as a dozen townships, and some data are organized by sections, of which there may be as many as thirty-six in a single township. Under such a system the collection of documentary material is logistically complicated.[15]

Similarly, because the farm population is well spread out, face-to-face interviewing cannot be conducted in the same way as it is in urban areas. Fewer interviews can take place in a working day, and scheduling must be flexible. Some rural sociologists resolve the logistical problems by employing a telephone or mailed, self-administered questionnaire.[16] Here, however, a number of important considerations ruled against this method of data collection. First, the best source for reconstructing a probability sample of intergenerational family farmers, the target group of the study, was unavailable. The records of the Agricultural Stabilization and Conservation Service are ideal for this task, but the agency's burdensome administration of the controversial farm program throughout the period of the study made it impractical for an independent researcher to use these materials. In any event, courthouse records and plat maps made satisfactory substitutes, given the specific nature of the target population and the need for as much face-to-face interaction with farm families as practical.

In view of these considerations and the fact that a single individual cannot hope to interview more than several dozen farm families, a number of compromises had to be reached. Since it was impossible to select a randomly drawn probability sample from all over the state, I used a multistage convenience sample of families with at least two generations farming together. Statistical rigor in selecting respondents was of less import here than the need to gather a rich variety of experiences, one-on-one, at the grass-roots level.[17]

Although logistics limited access to all but a few study areas, it was important to broaden the base of operations as much as possible. Therefore, farm families were interviewed in four different counties. In two, Fayette and Benton, archival work, participant observation, and some interviewing was begun before 1985 when I moved to Iowa permanently. This research continued systematically throughout 1986 and into 1987. In the fall of 1986 and winter of 1986-87 families in the two northwest counties of Ida and Sac were interviewed.

In each location every effort was made to become familiar

with the neighborhood and the families living there before contact took place. Mortgages, deeds, probate, property tax records, and the civil court docket were examined in the county courthouse and in private abstract companies. Bankruptcy was under federal jurisdiction, and no official record was kept in the county; therefore, I made several visits to the bankruptcy court for the northern district of Iowa in order to compile a list of farm bankruptcies in each county. I also sought out key informants knowledgeable about intergenerational farms in the area. From this preliminary research, I drew up a list of potential families from each county. After they were sorted by size of farm, locality, and degree of economic distress, the families were contacted to see whether they were willing to participate. In the end 135 families were interviewed; the questions they were asked and the method for coding their responses can be found in Appendixes B and C. Data collection methods are outlined in Appendix A.

Farmers are fortunate in not having to keep rigorous schedules. While many complained that the farm crisis had taken the fun out of farming, most had far more freedom than the average urban employee to do what they pleased. This scheduling flexibility was an advantage to a researcher who requested an interview. Farmers were used to laying whatever they were doing aside and "visiting" with salesmen on a call. At the same time, though willing to "philosophize" all afternoon about the state of the economy, the mess in Washington, or the Chicago Cubs, Iowa farmers were a good deal less willing to sit down and discuss their own personal affairs with a stranger. Farmers are loyal to their communities, and although they enjoy gossiping with one another, they are careful to avoid divulging information to outsiders about either themselves or their neighbors. Hence, it was especially important to lay good groundwork before contact. Key informants in the community, such as retired farmers, clergy, school principals, extension agents, and agribusinessmen, sometimes were solicited to provide access to a particular family. One telephone call usually smoothed the way.

At a time of great stress and even paranoia for certain families, it was not surprising that some potential interviewees were suspicious. Some believed that the visitor who appeared in their yard was yet another emissary sent by the bank to intimidate them. Ironically, the majority of those who refused to be interviewed were families that did not have financial problems; they were often those in the neighborhood with a reputation of being "tight." Having ridden out the farm crisis, they had bought or were just about to buy land. Not surprisingly, they were reluctant to show their hand to the world.

Quite the opposite response occurred with families who had gone through the mill of bankruptcy, foreclosure, and litigation. They had, as it were, come out of the closet and with few exceptions were willing to ignore any inhibitions they had in discussing their experiences. The intimate details of their financial and personal affairs were on public display. Some even produced their federal income tax returns to demonstrate the precariousness of their financial situation; others talked openly about their marital difficulties without prompting; still others broke down when recalling events of the past few years. Turndowns, fortunately, were rare. Only about twelve families refused to be interviewed. In general, whatever their economic circumstances, families seemed to welcome the chance to discuss their lives, their operations, and family involvement. Undoubtedly it gave them a new perspective on their situation.

Inasmuch as this was an intergenerational study, every effort was made to meet with all generations involved in an operation.[18] Sons (especially those under thirty) were sometimes difficult to track down. A number had left the farm to search for work out of state; some were away at college or were working long hours at some local off-farm job. Often in families whose head was in his late fifties or sixties, the elder generation dominated the interview. Fathers in retirement were more inclined to defer to their sons. Unfortunately, sex roles prevented me from having more interaction with farm wives, particularly daughters-in-law. Nevertheless, there were a number of strong women in the sample whose lives were profoundly altered by the farm crisis. They often made interviews a moving and learning experience.

The weather, scheduling, and a host of other factors prevented dual interviews on some occasions. In addition, the state of modern agriculture did not make participant observation of farm work easy. Fieldwork is crowded into a short time span during the year. The best opportunities for lengthy contact in work situations came among livestock farmers, especially dairymen and cattlemen who still made their own hay. Even an unskilled visitor could make a contribution by helping stack hay on a wagon or in the barn. Similarly, "walking beans," or picking up rocks forced above the soil by winter frosts in soybean fields, gave an opportunity to demonstrate some solidarity with a particular family and permitted long hours of observation and interaction. Wherever it was feasible, participant observation was the best way to arrive at a fair classification of a family for analytical purposes. Housing, farm machinery, food (in the home and in the field), automobiles, computer use, and furnishings could be observed and the knowledge added to data about economic behavior in the public record, family history, and attitudes to build up a picture.

I developed a more permanent relationship over some months with a dozen or so families, especially in the two eastern counties, Benton and Fayette, where I had been doing fieldwork for four years or more. Moreover, in all localities I participated in community activities such as sports events, county fairs, town open days, church services, farm sales, pork producer cookouts, young farmer club activities, as well as farm activist meetings.

The Grass-Roots Setting

The families in this study, then, while in no way representative of the state as a whole, are a reasonable approximation of a very important segment of the farm population: farmers with larger holdings, sales from $40,000 to $500,000 and more per year, who rely on family involvement in the business and who until the farm crisis rarely worked off the farm. To a considerable extent they constituted the segment of agriculture at greatest risk, for the pressures to expand in the 1970s fell most heavily on intergenerational operations. One other important characteristic should be noted. These families were far more likely to have mixed operations than was usual for an Iowa farm in the late seventies and eighties. With several family members to keep busy it was financially rational to have a mix of enterprises.

In addition, the agriculture in the four counties remained

diversified, for although farms grew larger throughout the seventies and row crops received greater emphasis, hogs continued to show strength in all localities. Cattle, however, slipped from prominence to some extent. At the same time, there was some variability in the scale of operations within each county.

In Fayette, for instance, there were several townships of stable population and relatively small, extremely diversified farms. In the southern part of the county, the old subsistence operations were eliminated in the fifties, when the land was tiled out. In their place came larger operators, often with large, modernized hog facilities.

In contrast much of Ida County in northwest Iowa is high, rolling country. By the 1930s the land was ravaged by soil erosion. Since World War II terracing has eliminated some of the worst abuses of farming hilly land. Nevertheless, the relatively poor land ensured that cow-calf operations and hogs and cattle retained their importance when other areas turned to grain farming in the seventies.

Next door, the west side of Sac has a tradition of larger farms going back to the nineteenth century. Long rolling slopes and well-drained land allowed big operations of several thousand acres before World War I. In this area, one of the largest farms in the state functioned on a grand scale until the 1970s. This was cattle-feeding country. For generations farmers had brought cattle from the West to be fattened on Iowa corn and shipped to the stockyards in Sioux City.

In Benton County, over a hundred and forty miles to the east, cattle feeding was also a major enterprise in some townships. In other areas the very productive soil encouraged the introduction of seed corn in the sixties. Farmers grew this crop under contract for major seed companies. In areas with less fertile land, smaller, mixed operations predominated.

A large percentage of the population of these counties directly depended on agriculture for their livelihood. Sac, Ida, and parts of Fayette were located at least fifty miles from the nearest metropolitan area, and although Benton was within thirty miles of Cedar Rapids and Waterloo, several of the largest employers in both communities were hard hit by the downturn of the farm economy. In the middle eighties Oelwein in Fayette lost almost a third of its population because of layoffs in the John Deere plant in Waterloo and other farm-related closings. Scores of houses in the town, often bought with Farmers' Home Administration mortgages, lay empty. Other communities were fortunate to have attracted light industry with little or no connection to farming. In Ida Grove the largest employer made paving equipment, which was exported all over the world. One of the factories in West Union made luggage for the Land's End catalog house.

But these businesses were exceptions in towns where agriculture directly or indirectly employed much of the labor force. In such places the health of the economy was tied to the health of farming. Once the downturn came, the anchor businesses that catered to the farm trade—the banks, hardware stores, and implement dealers—became as vulnerable to failure as their farmer customers.

To learn, then, how a rural society undergoes rapid economic change in the twentieth century, to capture the atmosphere of the farm crisis in Iowa, and to probe farmer behavior and reaction to the downturn, this book follows a rough chronology of the years 1975 through 1987. Most of the data comes from interviews with farm families in the sample, but where appropriate, it is supplemented from other sources. The first chapter places the farm family within the larger sphere of food production in the corn belt. It discusses how the family unit had to change as the structure of agriculture altered over the past thirty years. The next two chapters rely mostly on the survey data to explore the boom of the seventies and the beginnings of the downturn. Chapter 4 breaks away from the farmers themselves to look at the mobilization that turned the tide of the farm crisis at the state and local level. Chapter 5 considers the effect of the downturn on individual sample families and how they coped with an altered situation. And finally, before some conclusions are reached, a penultimate chapter explores why certain sample families suffered only slightly.

1

Structure

Throughout the twentieth century agriculture has been undergoing a modernization whose primary goal is the substitution of technology for human labor. Supporters of modernization see agriculture as a business and believe that, like any other industry, it is driven by the profit motive. This philosophy stands in opposition to an agrarian tradition whose advocates believe strongly that farming is a way of life and that the people who live on the land, and the land itself, should be given highest priority in the formulation of policy.

In the past twenty-five years modernization proceeded rapidly, and the power of agribusiness grew considerably. Great changes occurred in the structure of agriculture, nowhere more so than in the distance put between those who grew food and fiber and those who served farmers or manufactured the final product for the consumer. A few large corporations came to control the grain trade, and increasingly these firms bought up companies that supply fertilizers, herbicides, and seed. In the seventies, oil and chemical companies began to buy up sectors of the food-processing industry in order to capture a share of the new industry based on agrigenetic technology. The newly created divisions of these corporations possessed the power to consolidate food production into even fewer hands. By the middle seventies large agribusinesses, and chemical and pharmaceutical companies accounted for as many inputs in the production of farm commodities as farmers themselves. Similarly, the growing sophistication of agricultural service industries, such as finance, marketing, and computing, widened the gap between farmers and those who offered them services.[1]

By the seventies the structure of agriculture was also divided into several tiers. The first was the government in Washington, which had played a significant role in farming since the thirties.

Its role would grow more important in the eighties. A second tier consisted of a technologically driven sector composed of nationally and internationally based agribusiness firms (grain companies, meat packers, chemical manufacturers, etc.). The third and fourth tiers were agri-finance and educational institutions such as the land-grant colleges. A fifth was composed of establishment farm organizations (the Farm Bureau and National Corn Growers Association) and farm cooperatives, which though they were nominally controlled by local membership were affiliated with large parent cooperatives such as Land of Lakes. Finally came the producers of food and fiber, the farmers and ranchers themselves. Large organizations like seed companies, meat packers, machinery manufacturers, and the government reached down into the local community through salesmen, dealers, and agents. This system had a tendency to confuse loyalties and made the relationship between farm families and agribusiness more complex in a time of economic stress.

It would be disingenuous, however, to claim that the farm population itself is an undifferentiated mass. Sharp divisions exist among farmers and ranchers in the character of their operations, their educational levels, the time spent on the job, and their desire to modernize. Even among the sample families in this study—a select group to start out with—there were divisions.

While rural Iowa was an especially tricky locale in which to classify farmers by status, and the downturn further blurred differentiation, three groups could be distinguished in the sample. There was a tiny group of well-educated upper-class families (n = 8), in which both husband and wife had college degrees. They were usually more cosmopolitan in their professional and social contacts. Their world stretched farther than the village and clan orientation of their neighbors, who often farmed as much ground and had comparable assets. The second group (n = 108)—the vast majority of these two-generation farm families—came out of a tradition of stability and long-term ownership in their communities. Their families had lived in the neighborhood for several generations; they were often related to half a dozen other families round about; and their frugality and stability were rewarded until 1981 by the steady increase in the worth of their land. The third group (n = 19) came from a less stable tradition, often a tenant background; their families had moved around during the Depression and its aftermath. With little assistance from parents, they had had to make their own way, utilizing borrowed capital. Their desire to bring children into farming in the seventies made them especially vulnerable to possible economic dislocation.

Some have argued that the waste of human capital—the failure of the best and brightest in farming—could have a severe impact on local communities and leave agriculture as a whole in a less competitive position.[2] The "missing generation" thesis will be given some attention later; what needs to be underlined here is that some of the master farmers in the state of Iowa found that they had ceased to be the masters of their own destinies. The actual producers of food had allowed themselves to become the handmaidens of the idea of big agriculture, which fostered expansion through the use of large amounts of credit, undue attention to monoculture, and the substitution of machinery for labor. The technological and financial segment of food production—lenders, the grain trade, chemical companies, machinery manufacturers, government, and educators—so dominated the industry by the late seventies that there was little in the way of opposition to offer alternatives.[3]

How did this state of affairs come about, and what effect did this unequal relationship between farmers and the government and agribusiness have on the downturn? This chapter places farm families in the context in which they operated in the late seventies and early eighties and explores their relationships to the large institutions that catered to them.

Historical Trends

Corn-belt agriculture was integrated into national markets almost from the time the Midwest was settled. Grain and livestock prices fluctuated according to national and international events: wars were particularly profitable for Iowa farm families, whose products sharply increased in price during world conflicts. Unlike farmers in the wheat belt, who had to ship their grain very long distances and were beholden to variable transportation costs, corn-belt farmers usually fed their grain to their own animals and sold their livestock to terminal markets within 250 miles of the shipping point. Nevertheless, even though the farm family was dependent on outside forces for transportation, credit, and marketing, it remained physically isolated on its homestead. Most farm inputs were furnished by the family. The farm provided a third of its own food needs. Even education for the children was supplied through local resources in thousands of small school districts whose one-room schools were supported by real estate taxes and controlled by the immediate neighborhood.

The traditional family unit lived on land it could work with family labor and horse power. It employed a foolproof circular system—growing crops that were fed to livestock whose manure was then spread on the land. Before the introduction of chemical fertilizers and pesticides, strict crop rotation rejuvenated the soil and nature took care of pest control. In order to grow crops and raise animals on a 160-acre farm, the family head often had to toil twelve hours a day in summer and nine hours in winter, with the remainder of the family undertaking as much as 25 percent of the work load. Wives usually kept poultry flocks, did some of the milking, and planted and looked after the garden. Children worked at farm and household tasks as their age permitted. As late as the 1930s many wanted large families because of their labor value.[4]

The collapse of farming in the Great Depression brought change. Agriculture saw the beginnings of encroachment by government and other large organizations. First came government programs designed to cut production and raise income. Later, agribusiness began to influence the way crops were grown and livestock was raised. Slowly farm families became more dependent on outside inputs to make a living. The introduction of hybrid corn in the late thirties, the availability of electricity, the use of hydraulics, tractors, and other more sophisticated machinery, the discovery of antibiotics had produced a revolution in corn-belt agriculture by the forties. Although there was never an official policy of rural development, farmers migrated into urban occupations with increasing frequency in the late forties and fifties. They took advantage of jobs in farm-related industries like meat packing, agricultural implements, and grain processing. Out-migrants sold out to neighbors, and farms grew large enough to make efficient use of farm machinery. Industrialization was furthered to increase feed grain production for export out of the immediate area. The leveling and tiling of hitherto unproductive land and the introduction of larger machinery, improved strains of seed, and chemical fertilizers and pesticides helped increase both productivity and size of farms. For many farm families, the fifties were a time of transition. Specialization in one or two enterprises became common, and diversification as a means of risk avoidance was given less emphasis. Farmers pursued part ownership—owning some land but renting more—as one method of growing larger.[5]

It was no longer easy to begin farming without assistance from relatives, and young men who wanted to farm needed considerable monetary and in-kind help in order to begin a farm career. Modernization continued apace from 1954 through 1974, but the Extension Service and the agricultural press, which had dominated the diffusion of techniques in earlier decades, were supplanted by agribusiness. Seed, feed, and machinery dealers influenced farmers' attitudes, the way they farmed, and even how they spent their leisure. This trend was succinctly symbolized by farmers' wholesale adoption of baseball caps emblazoned with the logos of companies with which they did business.

To illustrate this gradual but appreciable change in farming in the recent past, Table 1 shows the increase in farm size in the regions in Iowa where this study took place. The important trend was not acreage increase. Farms grew, but not at a great rate. Rather, the most marked change was the increase in the amount of land devoted to row crops, even in three regions where diversified farming was still strong. As was noted earlier, the modernization of the hog industry kept it strong and growing across Iowa, but competition from the West and heavy losses produced a decline in cattle production over the period.

Unquestionably, agriculture has changed drastically in the twentieth century, but farmers for the most part have resisted modernization at every turn. During the Progressive era, they were slow to take up the challenge of the Country Life move-

Table 1. Average Acreage and Livestock per Farm, by Region, 1971-1983

Year	Acres per Farm	Acres per Farm in Row Crops	Pigs Weaned per Farm	Cattle Sold per Farm
		Northwest Iowa		
1971	289	198	448	182
1973	302	227	408	215
1975	304	233	472	172
1977	373	293	627	271
1979	360	307	607	142
1981	365	205	611	144
1983	366	320	718	99
		Northeast Iowa		
1971	274	158	364	44
1973	280	176	320	29
1975	279	209	304	30
1977	335	230	491	48
1979	333	281	614	49
1981	347	299	453	69
1983	335	289	791	27
		East Central Iowa		
1971	289	176	441	49
1973	295	202	356	44
1975	292	248	273	35
1977	367	279	542	57
1979	382	313	649	48
1981	398	358	641	42
1983	370	320	599	35

Source: Cooperative Extension Service, Iowa State Univ., Iowa Farm Costs and Returns (Ames, 1972-84).

ment.[6] Later, in the 1950s the diffusion of new techniques for animal production, such as routine use of antibiotics, took several years.[7] Thus, the expansion that occurred in the seventies, when land was bought, livestock enterprises expanded, elaborate buildings constructed, machinery purchased, and homes built and remodeled, was something of an aberration in farmer behavior and a tribute to the persuasiveness and growing influence of agribusiness. That the end result would be disaster for thousands of so-called progressive farmers in the mid-1980s underlined the gulf that separate those engaged in the production of food in the field—the family farmer—and those continuing and completing the process of bringing food to the table, in the bank, office, packing plant, factory, and supermarket.

Family Farming

Why has family farming been so durable in the corn belt? A number of scholars have offered explanations for its long domination, despite the great changes in other areas of the food-production chain. The most important reason has to do with what some have called the dialectic of the family farm.[8] The farm family, after all, provides its own labor and management, to a great extent controlling its own destiny. In short, it is very flexible. Decisions about investment and consumption are made internally and not by some manager hundreds of miles away. A sudden drop in wages and a period of frugality instituted for benefits in the long term are easily understood by family members, but less so by hired hands. This adaptability is valuable because farming is at the mercy of the weather and market cycles; and timing is crucial. The inherent risks have made farming less attractive to large, bureaucratic business interests, but farmers have learned to accept the rewards and risks as they come. Every day is a new day on the farm, and rigid timetables are given little priority except in caring for livestock. Farmers remain generalists in a world of increasingly narrow job descriptions. They are managers, laborers, mechanics, and veterinarians. When problems occur they must deal with them directly and immediately. There are no staff channels of communication to follow. Despite relatively low monetary returns, farming provides many

intangible rewards for the family. The vaunted independence of
farmers should not be scoffed at. Farmers are among the few
allowed to work at their own pace and to retain a self-image
"rooted in a sense of self mastery."[9]

Because of its unique configuration, blending work and family roles, the farm family has always needed a special chemistry
to operate successfully.[10] Indeed, it could be argued that the key
ingredient for success is the willingness to engage in self-exploitation. The constant need to care for animals and to perform
hundreds of mundane tasks in unpleasant conditions requires a
special dedication. Those not raised to follow such a regimen
might find this ethic of hard work difficult to tolerate. Not
surprisingly, farming has always been an occupation passed on
from generation to generation in a family.

By the 1970s, full-time farm operators like the ones studied
here had become a kind of landed gentry as rising land prices
gave them considerable wealth, on paper at any rate. For the first
time, there was some equality in status among small-town businessmen, professionals, and farmers. At the same time, there was
an increasingly large gulf in small service communities between
these three groups and those small-town residents who labored
for wages. The latter would be particularly hard hit once the
recession in agriculture hit Main Street.

The rapid changes that occurred in corn-belt agriculture
from the fifties onward—the gradual switch to grain farming, the
use of large machinery, and more specialized and efficient livestock management—tended to deemphasize the work ethic and
to steer families away from the kind of self-absorption in farm-
related tasks that so characterized earlier decades. A number of
phenomena began to have an impact on the structure and organization of the farm family. First, family cooperation between
generations became more popular, eventually leading to the
formalization of farm organization into partnerships and family
corporations. Estate planning became more important as land
prices rose and created a need to shelter heirs from estate tax
burdens.[11] Wives began to be involved in decision making in a
new way; younger couples and those with larger farms formed
what might be called husband-and-wife teams. According to one
observer, it was quite common for women to act as business

managers. "It used to be that wives came into our office to sign mortgages without knowing what's going on. Now they not only know, they are an important link in making it work." The likelihood of such participation depended, he said, "on how chauvenist the husband might be. Some men don't let loose the reins to the wife, or the children, for that matter."[12]

Technological progress allowed women to contribute in a different way from that of fifty years before. They drove tractors and assisted with livestock raising, as well as taking part in more traditional activities.[13] These changes tended to make the larger farm, particularly those with an intergenerational dimension, resemble a small urban business concern, while retaining its unique ability to meld work and family roles.

Intergenerational cooperation among farm families had gone on in Iowa for many generations, but it had sometimes been a struggle to make a smooth transition from one generation to another.[14] The pressures of production agriculture made the task no easier. Research in the seventies tended to emphasize the friction in families over power and authority,[15] conflict that was exacerbated by the increase in the value of land. With land selling for several thousand dollars an acre, many families became millionaires on paper, and very often the larger the stakes, the greater the conflict. Off-farm heirs and women were more likely to exert their rights than was previously the case.[16]

The desire to bring family members into an operation as full working partners required a number of strategic decisions. The family had to decide whether to expand and how. Should they buy more land, more livestock, or both; should they rent more acres? Should they finance expansion with a private contract, a long-term loan from the Land Bank, or funds accumulated by the family over many years? Finally, should the organization of the operation change in any way? These were just some of the questions to be answered. Some families looked at their options and went their separate ways. Sons farmed by themselves and worked with parents and other relatives only when the need arose. Others formalized their business relationships into partnerships, with strictly drawn lines of ownership, rental, and income. Still others opted for a closely held corporation, in which land, machinery, and other assets were pooled under a corporate umbrella, and shares were issued to family members in proportion to their involvement in the running and ownership of the farm.

One advantage of a family corporation was that it eliminated the concern a family had for heavy estate tax penalties when the elder generation died. The steady inflation of land values in the seventies made this an issue among farmers, and just before the downturn their lobbying efforts were rewarded. The passage of legislation incorporated into the Economic Recovery Act of 1981 greatly increased exemptions, lowered land values for the calculation of the tax, and made estate taxes payable over many years. By 1985, with land values plunging markedly, these changes no longer made much difference. Even so, some families could point to the payment of high estate taxes as one reason for their demise in the farm crisis.[17]

Much of the expansion in the seventies was undertaken with the younger generation in mind. Researchers have noted that sons and especially daughters-in-law often found their position in an intergenerational farm operation unsatisfactory. The daughter-in-law was particularly vulnerable in that she often had to maintain a far closer physical relationship with her in-laws than was the case in a nonfarm family. Sometimes she did not come from a farm background. The difficulties were complicated when two or more married sons were farming together, and sibling rivalries as well as intergenerational differences emerged. Income division, schedules, vacations, and the purchase of expensive consumer items could all cause contention among family members. Daughters-in-law could be entirely left out of major strategic decisions, such as the purchase of land.[18] The younger generation, unless it was a full partner in an operation, felt less secure because the seniors usually owned most of the land and retained much management control.[19] Not surprisingly, when the downturn hit and an intergenerational operation seemed headed for failure, the young proved more willing to abandon farming and seek other employment.

The elderly are in an especially strategic position in farm families because of their continued control of land after they retire. In some townships in this study elderly women owned up to one-third of all tracts of land—testimony not only to their longevity but also to how the inheritance system operated. On small and medium-sized farms the usual method of taking care of a spouse after the death of her husband was to provide her with a life estate on a parcel of land. The rental from the land gave her an annuity for the rest of her life. Farmland was an ideal vehicle for this purpose, for the steady rise in land prices correlated with that of rents. By the seventies elderly widows were being handsomely reimbursed by tenants eager to rent more land. It was not unusual for a 160-acre tract to gross between fifteen and twenty thousand dollars in yearly income for the owner. Such sums were impressive particularly if they were invested in savings accounts paying high interest. No wonder the elderly sometimes relished their power over their younger relatives. Some indulged a kind of gamesmanship over sons and daughters who were interested in renting and inheriting land.[20] The attitude of elderly landowners in a climate of high land prices and inflation had an important bearing on the way many families operated.

Business Relationships

Some national figures that chart change in the number of inputs farmers utilized over the past sixty years illustrate how farming has moved from relative self-sufficiency to dependence on outside sources. In 1920 exactly half of all inputs on the farm were made up by the labor of the family itself, with machinery providing almost 12 percent and chemicals 2 percent. By 1980 machinery made up one-third of all inputs; meanwhile labor had fallen to only 14 percent of the total, and chemicals had increased to 11 percent.[21] By the late 1970s most of the resources needed to farm came from the outside.

In order to run a farm in the seventies, the typical two-generation family had both a long- and a short-term lender. The former was often the Land Bank, although it could be an insurance company. In addition, a certain percentage of land was bought on contract from individuals—often parents or other close relatives. Short-term lending for routine operations had a more varied base, with local banks being the main source. However, as families expanded they often outgrew the lending limits of the smaller country banks. The Production Credit Association within the Farm Credit System took over the business that required larger lines of credit in the short term. The lender of last resort, the Farmers' Home Administration, had less involvement with larger operations before the late seventies, but as the economy worsened, loan guarantees were introduced, and lending policies became more stringent, larger farmers turned to the FmHA more often. Infrequent visits to the bank to make principal and interest payments were usually the only contact a farmer had with a loan officer. Paperwork in planning a loan and assessing a client's ability to repay was minimal. In small local banks overdrafts were common, and one telephone call from a customer was enough to cover the purchase of livestock which in many cases had already occurred. The key elements here were a trusting relationship built up between the parties over an extended period of time and the ever-increasing equity of a farmer's land, which provided the collateral for the borrowed funds. At the same time, the Depression experience gave farmers a fear of going deeply into debt. Generally they repaid their loans on time, and there were universally good relations between farmers and lenders before the eighties.[22]

Farmers had financial obligations with a number of other businesses in the local area. These included notes for machinery purchases, and accounts at the feed and seed store. Feed bills were normally taken care of through regular thirty-day payments. In the boom local merchants, like bankers, were liberal in extending credit, even though much of it, unlike bank loans, was unsecured. When a reversal in the farm family's fortunes came, there was no collateral to cover a merchant's losses.

As price "takers" rather than price "makers," farmers sold their grain to the elevator and their livestock to the packer or collection point and took the going price. While there was some flexibility in where livestock or grain could be sold, for the most part, farmer autonomy in marketing decisions was an illusion. By the seventies, government programs and the intrustion into the grain business of the Board of Trade and a handful of multinational corporations were largely responsible for grain pricing. The concentration of cattle feeding in the vast lots of the plains and Southwest and the continued turmoil of the meat-packing industry in the seventies and eighties did not work in farmers' favor. The risk involved in marketing farm products also had an important bearing on farmers' ability to make money. The rapid computerization of futures trading revolutionized agricultural marketing and placed the average farmer at an even greater disadvantage compared to large institutional players. A farm family's ability to hedge its risks both through diversification of product and on the Board of Trade and Mercantile Exchange often had a bearing on performance. Unfortunately, many farmers used these newer methods to hedge and speculate unwisely and only added to their woes.

The boom allowed farm families and local agriculture-related business to make more money—at least before expenses were paid. Old ways of operating were sometimes forgotten in order to take advantage of the bonanza conditions that prevailed for a few years. The world food crisis of the seventies suggested that farmers, like oilmen, possessed considerable power. In the words of one ebullient editor, there was "a new realization by farm people of the vast economic power they have abroad as well as at home."[23] Such sentiments by a cheerleader for what was called the "new era for agriculture," masked the true picture of where farm families stood with their business partners once the boom collapsed.

Finance and Education

One of the roles of the land-grant university is to train young people—particularly farm children—to assume positions in agricultural extension, finance, and agribusiness. The people so trained, though often from a farm background, have distanced themselves from the land; they have different loyalties and values from those of the farmers they are meant to serve. In the words of Wendell Berry, these kinds of jobs "were a means to escape farming," not to serve farmers. Those who took this route were "old farm boys," who, it was said, had gone "on to better things."[24] In Iowa there is a strong connection between lending institutions and Iowa State University, the land-grant college, which also administers the Cooperative Extension Service. Hundreds of graduates with agricultural education degrees have gone into positions in private banks, the Farm Credit System, and the Farmers' Home Administration. While the land-grant college graduates do not possess a monopoly of these jobs, the fact remains that no industry is more inbred than agriculture and agribusiness, and the old-farm-boy land-grant network reaches deeply into all corners of agri-finance and agribusiness. The brain drain from farming by this route is nothing new. Nevertheless, at a time when agriculture required more ability in finance and marketing than ever before, much of its homegrown talent sat on the other side of the desk from the farmer and pushed loans, larger machinery, and the illusion of wealth across to those who still grew the crops and raised the livestock.

Rural banking, like agriculture, witnessed great changes in the decade of the seventies. Banking was severely regulated in the Depression. Interest rates were pegged to savings accounts, and country lenders were largely isolated from national financial developments. They mostly relied on internal sources of capital to finance investment in livestock and equipment by farmer borrowers. The Land Bank provided much of the long-term credit for agriculture at interest rates of 5 percent or a little less. By the end of World War II, funds for this purpose were generated by borrowers themselves through stock purchases. Government sources for loans through the Farmers' Home Administration were severely restricted and regulated.

This conservatively run and stable business climate was destroyed with the deregulation of banking in the seventies. During that decade banks were allowed to utilize money market mutual funds and certificates of deposit for the first time. Customers took advantage of these changes by switching their deposits from low-yielding savings accounts to the more profitable investments, whose annualized yields often exceeded 10 percent. As a result rural banks lost their old reliable source of the funds that had traditionally been used for agricultural loans. The new sources of funds were more expensive. As banks paid out higher and higher interest to depositors, they charged their farmer borrowers correspondingly higher rates. The deregulation that revolutionized banking all over the country had an especially insidious effect on agricultural lenders.[25]

Competition between banks had not been a factor in the past.

Interest rates were uniform, and farmers generally supported their local bank because it was convenient. In the 1970s, however, lenders began to seek out new customers. The Farm Credit System and later the FmHA became competitive with commercial banks to attract new accounts. Dangerous practices, rare in the days of strict regulation, such as pyramiding long-term on short-term debt, became common. These questionable transactions, based on inflated land values, collapsed as soon as land prices fell, and lenders began to demand a balance sheet with what in the business was called "a healthy cash flow."

During the boom, lenders seemed like partners to farmers, and often they encouraged the plunging binge. Two illustrations should be sufficient to demonstrate the kind of reckless policies adopted by both commercial institutions and those supported by tax dollars. During the seventies and early eighties, the Hawkeye Bank Corporation, a Des Moines–based holding company took advantage of the Iowa law that permitted branch banking. The bank grew until it owned an interest in thirty-six banks around the state, many of them in questionable condition. The bank pursued a deliberate plan to purchase agricultural banks between 1978 and 1982.[26] By 1984 these agricultural banks were beginning to suffer severe losses. In 1985 the holding company was teetering on the brink of bankruptcy, and its affairs were being overseen by a review committee appointed by its creditors. Between January and September 1985 Hawkeye lost more money ($83.8 million) than it had made during the previous ten years combined. Ten of its banks were put up for sale in an effort to prevent further losses. Hawkeye's problems were partly caused by deregulation and the bonanza atmosphere it created, for its expansion was financed not from Iowa sources but from loans by large Chicago banks and insurance companies around the country. These companies treated Iowa like another Latin America. Hawkeye bank officers in turn spurned the golden rule of bankers, which is to maintain reserves equal to 8 percent of assets.[27]

The Farmers' Home Administration, since the forties considered the "lender of last resort," also altered its style of lending in the seventies. In 1960 this agency administered eight national programs; 64 percent of its funds went to farm operating loans, and 14 percent to farm ownership loans with the remainder to other programs. By 1979 FmHA operated at least twenty-three programs, and farm ownership and operating loans had shrunk to under 10 percent of all funds dispensed. New programs now dominating the agency's portfolio included disaster emergency, economic emergency, housing, rural rental housing, water and waste, and business and industrial loans. Although absolute levels of funding for operating and ownership had not declined, the general perception of the agency had changed: it had become a major provider of subsidized credit and emergency loans. This policy tended to expand farmers' perceptions of their capacity to borrow money safely, encouraging them to pursue riskier production and marketing strategies and more aggressive financial plans. Thus while 50 percent of all farm operation loans in 1979 went to farmers below the age of thirty, and 68 percent of loans were dispensed to farms with less than $120,000 net worth, one-third of all emergency loans were given to farms with more than $500,000 in assets.[28]

In Iowa this policy was reflected in the middle eighties by the number of loans past due and the large amounts of some of these loans. For instance, in one sample county one past-due loan totaled over $700,000. In the two western counties of Ida and Sac 34 percent and 29 percent of FmHA agricultural borrowers were past due. Much of this delinquency was due to the livestock losses and crop failures farmers had suffered in the previous decade. Other counties, like Fayette, had very low agricultural losses, but their housing programs in the towns were under severe strain because mortgage holders had lost their jobs in agriculture-related industry.[29] The performance of the Farm Credit System in the 1970s and early 1980s duplicated many of these trends. The Omaha District, of which Iowa was part, suffered crippling losses after 1984.

Like the farmers, these lending institutions collapsed or were badly crippled when the boom ended. Many factors contributed to their failure; most obvious were actions by the Federal Reserve that caused the decline in inflation, the fall of farm prices, and the steep loss in the value of land. Lapses in judgment, bad management, and ill-advised expansion were all partly to blame. Certainly the deregulation that encouraged formerly conservative professionals to take risks had an important impact.

For many years the Cooperative Extension Service was a voice for change in the countryside. County agents pleaded with farmers to adopt modern techniques, and home economists did the same for farm women in the home. This missionary activity made its mark by the 1950s, but by then commercial firms had taken over many of the functions of the county agent and his staff. Commercial enterprises now held their own demonstrations, attracting farmers and their families with free meals and handouts of clothing, feed, and seed. At the same time the Extension Service pamphlet, used to such great effect in an earlier time, became outdated. It took several years for the institution to adopt new electronic techniques for mass instruction. As a result, under 30 percent of all Iowa farm households used the Extension Service on a regular basis by the mid-1970s.[30]

As an arm of the United States Department of Agriculture, the Extension Service had little alternative in the seventies but to follow the dictates of Washington and bolster big agriculture. Much work was done in estate planning, livestock confinement, new marketing techniques, and above all, pushing production agriculture to higher and higher levels. In light of what happened in the eighties, it is a pity that the service did not demonstrate more leadership and question some of the trends of the seventies. In its support of an agribusiness philosophy, the Extension Service forgot that one of its tasks was to give an objective appraisal of change in agriculture, not to lock step with agribusiness. Apparently farmers were aware of these developments, for according to an Iowa Poll, 34 percent thought the Extension Service was dedicated to serving agribusiness, whereas only 28 percent believed it looked after the interests of the family farmer.[31]

Extension paid too much attention to the needs of the larger production-oriented farm families and not enough to smaller and part-time operations. Ironically, in the farm crisis many of the plungers who had followed the gospel of big agriculture and, by inference, the Extension Service, were severely affected. A little later a clientele that desperately needed assistance in the worst period of the downturn—older farmers with smaller holdings—had considerable difficulty making contact with the service. They had either lost touch with the Extension Service years before or had never had a relationship with the county agent in the first place.

Agribusiness

Nowhere is the gap in financial and marketing expertise between the individual farmer-businessman and those who process his product more pronounced than in the huge multinational grain companies, the "merchants of grain," who came into their own in the seventies with the explosion in grain exports.[32] And no firm better characterizes the mysterious activities of the grain traders than the largest of them all, Cargill, the Minnesota giant that had $32 billion in revenues in 1986. Cargill originated in Iowa, but its founders quickly saw the importance of the Minnesota Twin Cities for the milling business and moved there before the turn of the century. By any standards Cargill is an extraordinary American business. It remains privately held, has been largely self-financed, and puts great stock in long-term strategic planning.[33]

Until the 1970s Cargill concentrated on the grain business and grew relatively slowly. However, in the next ten years the firm turned itself into the classic multinational conglomerate. Revenues of $2.1 billion in 1971 grew to $29 billion ten years later. The company diversified into fifty different bulk commodities—in the best of times a very risky enterprise. It became first in grain exports, egg production, and soybean crushing, second in beef packing, third in corn and wheat milling, a top cotton and coffee trader, and important in feed, seed, fertilizer, steel, wool, zinc, and corn syrup, as well as financial services. Cargill employed forty-two thousand people in forty-six countries and maintained its position by continued reinvestment in the firm and continued diversification. While grain exports slumped in the eighties, salt, animal feed, poultry, coffee, and financial services prospered. Nevertheless, inasmuch as Cargill exported 20 percent of the nation's grain in the early eighties, the farm slump and the problems of maintaining farm exports remained a concern.

Evidence came to light in the spring of 1987 that Cargill and other large grain companies were helping to orchestrate a defeat of legislation that would put controls on production and so raise prices for farmers. With its extensive lobbying apparatus in Washington, Cargill became a major player in the formation of the 1985 farm bill. Calling their efforts "a sham and a scandal," the president of the National Farmers Union declared, "These companies recognize that their profit is substantial and that it results from their handling of farm products. They are involved in a deliberate effort to force prices down. This is pure exploitation."[34]

Cargill claimed that its interests were the same as the farmers' and that its work in building up exports and keeping costs low in order to undersell competitors would help farmers. It would seem that the firm achieved the best of both worlds. The bill steered the economy toward "market clearing" prices that made American grain more attractive to foreign buyers. At the same time, though exports did not increase, Cargill and other grain merchants made large sums of money storing surplus commodities for the Commodity Credit Corporation.[35]

At first sight it would seem that the farm cooperative movement would run counter to the thesis that farmers are at the mercy of large-scale business organizations. The Rochdale system, adopted by hundreds of small farmer-owned cooperatives from the turn of the century onward, was designed to market crops and reduce the price of farm inputs for members by avoiding the middleman. However, by the seventies most cooperatives were affiliated with large parent institutions and were run like any other big business. AGRI industries, which was once called the Farmers'-Grain Dealers Association, grew into the largest grain cooperative in Iowa. Rapid expansion in the seventies was followed by substantial losses by the early eighties. The cooperative was saved only when Cargill bought 51 percent of its stock in 1986 with a view to runnng AGRI's main business, its grain market.[36] Such a turn of events showed elements of bitter irony, in that a farmer-owned business was forced to sell out to a commercial competitor, making a mockery of the concept of cooperation designed to reduce farmers' disadvantage in the grain trade. As in the debacle of the Farm Credit System—also nominally owned by farmer shareholders—when difficulties

arose in a large organization, it was the organization, not the
shareholders, that received most attention. Unfortunately, the
AGRI experience demonstrated the powerlessness of the farm
cooperative movement and its dominance by agribusiness.

Meat packing, another industry with close farm relations,
also underwent major structural changes in the past twenty-five
years. In 1947 the four biggest meat packers, Armour, Morrell,
Swift, and Wilson, accounted for 41 percent of the value of meat
added by manufacture. In 1963 this share had declined to 31
percent. By the seventies only one of these firms was still in
business, and slaughtering no longer took place in terminal
markets like Chicago, but in small, dispersed plants much closer
to where livestock was raised.[37]

Meat cutting is a tough occupation with a long history of
union militancy and strike activity. Since the movement of the
industry to smaller communities, unions have attempted to
organize plants in areas where antiunion sentiment was strong.
Their most important target was Iowa Beef Processors, or IBP, a
division of Occidental Petroleum, now the country's largest meat
packer. IBP has thirteen plants, four of them in Iowa, and all the
Iowa plants are nonunion. The company was able to take advantage of the need for jobs in a state where off-farm employment is
at a premium in small towns. With starting wages at $5.25 per
hour, the union has some justification in claiming that IBP is
"exploiting workers while making millions." IBP also was able
to use the "speedup" in the cutting line so graphically depicted
in Upton Sinclair's The Jungle. According to the union, which
said it had trouble documenting many of its facts because of the
intimidation of workers by the firm, the work force in many
plants had a turnover of 100 percent a year. In one new Iowa
location an average of forty workers a week left because conditions were "brutal." Some had knife wounds, ammonia burns, or
other injuries. To counter union influence, the company sent
new workers to an eight-hour orientation program designed to
present the company's program in the best light and to dis-
courage union sentiment.[38]

The IBP situation is indicative, albeit to an exaggerated degree, of the conditions in rural America in the deflationary slide
of the eighties. Workers want good wages, safe working condi-

tions, and the ability to raise a family in a small community. Management, employed by a huge absentee oil company, is concerned with profit maximization, with turning out nine hundred butchered hogs an hour, and paying the lowest possible wages for a work week that includes Saturdays.

The lack of work-force stability had consequences that went beyond the employees themselves, for although most Iowa communities were desperate for jobs, IBP's reputation as an employer made it difficult for the company to build other plants in the state. When the firm tried to set up a plant in an eastern Iowa community, opposition surfaced not only from townspeople but from farmers as well. Some were concerned that any more competition in the hog-slaughtering industry in their part of the state would lower prices for their product. Moreover, the farm crisis tended to cement relations between farmers and union members, and IBP's bad press made its mark, whereas a decade before farmers would likely have supported IBP's efforts at expansion.[39]

Other businesses close to farmers, such as implement dealers and their parent companies, the manufacturers, met disaster in the farm crisis. Their failure demonstrated the folly of a business mentality that stressed short-range profit in place of a balanced long-range sales program. Farmers had been persuaded to trade in tractors and other machinery once a year during the seventies, when capital was cheap. The practice was perfectly rational when the rate of inflation was higher than the cost of borrowing money; then, farmers bought tractors as an investment. Unfortunately, competition between dealers, and between lending institutions eager to write loans that would finance farm machinery, allowed some customers to make unwise purchases. As with expensive farmland bought on credit, once deflation occurred, many farmers could not keep up with their payments.[40]

In the 1970s tractor manufacturers possessed a special aura; farmers held them in high esteem. John Deere, for example, maintained 173 dealerships in the state and had 30 percent of the market for large machines. A typical dealer employed six mechanics and had annual sales of $1 million to $6 million, $250,000 in used inventory, and $80,000 in parts. Competition was keen not only with other kinds of dealerships, but within the Deere family itself.[41] Between 1980 and 1986 Iowa lost 265 implement dealers, and their attrition caused hardships to farmers, who not only lost the advantage of a competitive business climate but now had to drive far longer distances for repairs and service. The impact of the downturn in farm machinery sales was as severe in urban Iowa as the farm downturn was for small towns, for it entailed the loss of thousands of jobs in manufacturing plants located in Iowa cities.

The saga of Harvestores, the tall blue grain silos commonly to be found on livestock farms in the corn belt, was symbolic of the boom and bust that agribusiness firms experienced between 1975 and 1985. The Harvestore was a mark of status. Several in a row added even more prestige. In the boom years dealers organized Harvestore clubs for owners. Members attended steak dinners and went on tours to visit others who used the "Harvestore system." Potential customers were wooed with "seminars at sea" or trips to Las Vegas. According to one observer, "There was a sort of well-to-do air or 'country club' attitude among those who 'belonged.' " Five years later the world of "expensive blue" had turned to rust. In many instances, the Harvestore became the symbol of failure.[42]

In sum, agribusiness had a mixed record in the seventies and eighties. Some sectors suffered as much, if not more, than farmers. Those that had diversified under good management were not hurt as badly. But regardless of their record, their influence and power was such that farmers had little recourse but to meekly follow in their wake.

Farm Organizations

One of few farm organizations with any hope of competing with agribusiness, the National Farmers Organization, lost much of its credibility among larger more conservative farmers when it resorted to withholding products from the market in the fifties and sixties. Nor did the American Agriculture Movement attract much of a following in Iowa in the late seventies, partly because of the preeminence of the Iowa Farm Bureau Federation.[43] The Farm Bureau was formed just after World War I as an organizational and farm representative arm of the Cooperative Extension Service. Establishment oriented and conservative, the Farm Bureau achieved most of its success through such business activities as a group insurance program open to nonfarmers as well. Wary of federal farm programs, the bureau led the drive for "free-market" agriculture and even as late as 1985 continued to endorse this concept, while attempting to recoup its position, having lost face in the farm crisis.[44]

The bureau was slow to recognize and react to the farm crisis mainly because of its own conservatism. Traditionally it operated by consulting with its membership and reaching consensus before embarking on a change of policy. Many members, however, clearly did not want to recognize the symptoms of the downturn. Unlike other farm organizations, the Farm Bureau was relatively well-heeled. Membership fees of sixty dollars a year supported a national headquarters staff of two hundred, in addition to eight regional offices around the country. Like other mainstream farm organizations, such as the National Corn Growers Association and American Soybean Association, the Farm Bureau placed great emphasis on making its voice heard in Washington. In the 1980s it began endorsing political candidates, formed political action committees, and developed a computer information system called Speedline, which allowed members to communicate directly with Washington to express their views on important issues. Other Farm Bureau programs dealt with marketing information and education, and there were programs for women and children too. These, together with financial stability, gave it formidable strength and credibility compared to other farm organizations that challenged its hegemony.[45]

Still, for all its vigor, its ability to organize in every township in Iowa, and its strong voice in the state legislature, the Farm Bureau remained unpopular among farmers because of its business orientation. If critics claimed the bureau did not pay enough attention to the needs of dirt farmers, they were correct. But then, the Farm Bureau epitomized how the structure of agriculture had changed in twenty-five years, and how a business orientation had prevailed.

The Government

A good case could be made that government intervention was the principal force behind structural change in agriculture. Farm programs and tax policy are usually cited as instrumental in initiating change since the Depression and particularly after 1970. Historically, Iowa farmers did not make great use of farm programs. As late as 1954 farmers in the state voted down an option for the mandatory retirement of land. Farmers resented government dictation of policy, but perhaps more important, they believed the withdrawal of land would handicap the small farmers of the day. Most still fed much of their corn to livestock, and many feared that prices would rise if they had to buy corn for feed on the market.[46] Even in 1986 after the passage of the most controversial farm bill ever, the average payments to corn growers were relatively modest. The controversy concerned the legal ability of larger farmers to manipulate the rules of programs in order to receive the maximum payment possible. Larger operators were invariably able to take greater advantage of the farm program than the smaller operators, who needed support payments to retain economic viability. In Iowa, then, farm programs did not become a key issue until after 1980, and are best dealt with later.

Tax policy, on the other hand, had a fairly strong cumulative effect. The income tax system encouraged farmers to take advantage of depreciation and investment tax credits, instead of saving their excess income as they would have done a generation before. In addition, the system made it advantageous for nonfarmers to use farming as a tax shelter in the sixties and seventies. Nonfarmer investment damaged the Iowa cattle industry and influenced the westward migration of this important segment of the state's farm economy. Iowa farmers took advantage of provisions that allowed them to write off the costs of land improvement, the purchase of machinery, and the construction of buildings where livestock were reared. Generally the greater the income of a farmer, the higher the value of these tax code rules to his operation. There was a tremendous incentive to continue enlarging the farm and to substitute capital for labor, in order to reach income tax brackets that would be of maximum advantage to the farm family.[47]

In the 1970s, thus, large organizations assumed an increasingly powerful role, changing the structure of agriculture and deciding the direction farming would take. Urged by lenders, the government, and agribusiness, many operators undertook rapid modernization and expansion. Theirs was a rational approach, perhaps, in an inflationary environment, but the risks were great. Once a deflationary economy was triggered by a recession after 1981, disaster struck. Before turning to the experience of farm families in the downturn, it is important to explore the period of boom in greater detail.

2

Boom

In the late sixties and early seventies some farmers began to change the way they lived and worked. For years the experience of the Great Depression had influenced farm families. The image of the "frugal" farmer, someone who never bought anything unless he had the cash, died hard. But an inflationary economy gradually altered these attitudes for a segment of the farm population.

The Good Life and Its Costs

The idea that the good life could be had in rural America came to fruition in the 1970s. The steep increase in the price of corn and soybeans after the Russian grain deal of the early seventies, followed by the phenomenal rise in the price of land, brought new prosperity. Life-styles changed; family conflict was sometimes forced into the open; and the old stigmas against borrowing money were sometimes forgotten.

Nothing summarizes these years better for the Iowa two-generation farm family—at least in regard to the first two themes—than the evocative description by Calvin Trillin of the experience of the Hartman family, which exemplifies the human dilemma a rapid increase in landed wealth imposed on ordinary farm people. Though the tragic story is hardly typical, it usefully encapsulates the elements at play in the farm family in the time of unprecedented prosperity.[1]

Lawrence Hartman lived and farmed with his wife and two grown sons in the northern part of Grundy County, whose rich black soil is some of the most productive in the world. The family was of hardworking German stock, whose lives revolved round their families, their land, and their church. Lawrence had

taken over from his father in 1947, the year he married Esther
Meester, who came from one of the neighborhood's most prominent families. He began farming the 240 acres of the home place
in a fifty-fifty partnership with his father. Thirty years later he
would use the same arrangement with his own sons on their hog,
cattle, and grain operation.

Over the years the Hartmans' holdings grew steadily. Esther
inherited some land, but mostly their expansion was due to the
shrewd dealings of Lawrence, who bought ground when it was
cheap and saw it grow in value. Esther worked alongside her
husband from the beginning—not just running the home but
opening gates, helping with livestock, and keeping the books. In
short, she seemed to have inherited undiluted the values brought
to Iowa by the God-fearing, thrifty settlers from East Friesland.
She was strict about keeping the Sabbath and about having
liquor in the house. She still canned vegetables and baked pies
and cakes, and her home was always immaculate.

By 1977, with land selling at thirty-five hundred dollars an
acre, farmers like the Hartmans were sitting on a gold mine.
Their five hundred acres made them millionaires. Land was a
limited resource and there seemed to be no end to the increase in
its value. One evening Lawrence was having a drink with a cattle
buyer in a Cedar Falls cocktail lounge, when he fell into conversation with a thirty-year-old divorcee. Soon Lawrence began
to pay more attention to his girl friend than to his farm. In the
words of one of his sons, "He lost the ability to manage." He was
gone at crucial times, during planting, for example, and when
the hogs were farrowing. He even missed two consecutive Christ-
mases with the family. His indiscretions affected not only the
family itself but the business affairs and the routine operations of
the farm. As senior partner in an intergenerational business, he
could not absent himself from management without damaging
the operation. So intertwined were familial and work roles on
the family farm that the failures of husband and father were also
the failures of chief manager.

Esther, who was raised in a society where the permanence of
the marriage contract was unquestioned, sought counseling for
the couple. But after this failed, she began divorce proceedings
in the spring of 1980. In a month the estranged couple were back

together. Lawrence was contrite. He indicated that this chapter of his life was over, and Esther seemed to forgive him.

But on a stormy Saturday night in September Lawrence summoned their pastor to the house. There, the minister found Esther dead, all but one of her ribs broken, her lungs crushed. Hartman was in a daze. He said he had been out for the evening—at his girl friend's it turned out—and when he returned had found his wife dead at the foot of the basement stairs where she had fallen while bringing down the laundry.

That December, Hartman was indicted for the murder of his wife, and a few months later his sons brought a wrongful death suit against him in civil court. This action was aimed at blocking Lawrence's right to inherit his wife's part of the family property. At the murder trial Lawrence had some difficulty in explaining his whereabouts on the night in question, but because of lack of evidence, he was convicted of murder in the second degree.

How had a family man, a community leader, someone of unassailable reputation, fallen so far? Some said he was smitten, bewitched, obsessed by a younger woman who introduced this unworldly farmer to temptations he could not resist. Others said it was "cattle buying," where a grain and hog farmer strayed too far from his home turf. Still others, however, said Lawrence Hartman just could not cope with wealth. One of Lawrence's sons seemed to agree with this kind of logic. When asked what had happened, he answered with a single word: inflation.[2]

Indeed, Lawrence Hartman was not alone in his desire for wider horizons. In the mid-1970s a "bolder, richer and younger breed" of farmer appeared in the countryside. In the past farmers had hoarded every penny against the uncertainties of the future. Now they were enjoying their wealth. One central Iowa hog farmer raised eight thousand pigs a year, worked fifty hours a week, but took most of the weekends off in order to enjoy the fruits of his labor. As well as playing an occasional round of golf, he skied, snowmobiled, took flying lessons, and drove a Cadillac. He and his wife enjoyed a summer home in Minnesota and held a part ownership in a Florida mobile home. They took vacations in Jamaica, attended the Farm Bureau convention in Hawaii, and rebuilt old cars as a hobby. To them the gap between city and country people seemed to have narrowed. City people had been golfing for twenty years, "while I've been working," said the farmer. He compared himself to the president of a small corporation in town and felt he did not have to "apologize to anyone for doing well."[3]

One survey showed that farmers were adopting the urban style of "keeping up with the Joneses." Many became preoccupied with farm machinery, for a full line of well-kept, shiny new machinery was the most prestigious symbol in the pecking order.[4] But for all the flashy activity of the "young tigers," many Iowa farmers "did not do anything different than they did before." The rise in the value of land had made them millionaires, but until they sold their farms they had to live on corn and beans. The stereotypical Iowa farm millionaire wore bib overalls, drove a pickup, went to church, and had a daughter who taught Sunday school. For him the biggest game in town was two-bit pepper in the back room of the tavern. To be sure, there was evidence of prosperity in the spruced-up farmhouses, new lines of machinery—the old tractors "were worn out for tax purposes"—and longer winter vacations. Still, for many, money was not just spent because it was earned. Anyone who had been around farming any length of time remembered lean times and understood that there could very well be troubles ahead.[5]

Lenders and Borrowers

Without the cooperation and urging of lending institutions, farmers would not have been so ready to change their minds about the desirability of employing equity financing to expand. In more stable times loans were based on the earnings of the business, but during the inflationary 1970s, lenders based loans on net worth of farm assets, or even potential net worth of assets that seemed certain to rise in value. Lenders typically gave farmers who wished to expand more money than they required, counting on the ever-increasing price of land to cover the larger sums. The farm families in my sample found credit available for the asking, and no family that wanted to expand had trouble borrowing the necessary capital. The boom created fierce competition between lenders for farm customers. One conservative farmer, tempted by offers, admitted, "Even we could have got enough money to get ourselves in trouble." Aggressive solicitation, especially by the Farm Credit System, which was attempting to build up its agricultural portfolio at the expense of local banks, was commonplace.[6] According to one farmer, his local Production Credit Association "couldn't give enough money away." Indeed, both the Farm Credit System and the Farmers' Home Administration sometimes required a greater degree of expansion than the borrower requested, for with the economy booming it made better economic sense to build a larger hog-farrowing unit than was originally planned. The lender would reap greater returns in the form of bigger interest payments, and the borrower would benefit from having a larger operation. Once a staff was assembled at a branch office, it had to be kept busy. One day in the middle seventies a Farmers' Home Administration borrower received a call from his loan officer asking whether he could use more credit. The loan officer hoped that the answer was in the affirmative, "so that he could keep the staff on, and the office in business."

Some families used short-term obligations to cover long-term loan payments with the approval of lenders. Thus the local bank, Production Credit, or the Farmers' Home Administration provided funding for operating expenses, which the farmer used to pay interest and principal on thirty-year mortgages from the Federal Land Bank. It was a questionable practice, acceptable during a period of high inflation perhaps, and it proved a burden when the economy moved towards a deflationary cycle. Living expenses, home remodeling and construction, and consumer items, which were not vital to the operation of the farm, were dependent on the whim of the short-term and long-term lender, ensuring that some operations were exceedingly vulnerable once the storm broke. The boom encouraged many to live beyond their means. "With a brand new pickup and snowmobile in the back, you were good for a loan," as one farmer described the consumption-oriented seventies.

Some farmers routinely required large amounts of operating money to run their businesses. Cattle feeders, for example, brought young cattle into their feedlots, kept them for several months, and then sold them for slaughter. In the late seventies and early eighties extremely high inflation paralleled a downturn in the cattle market. In order to stay in business, feeders were forced to borrow large amounts of money at high interest rates. Table 2 shows the borrowing behavior of five farmers in my Benton County sample in this period. All were cattle feeders in their forties and fifties, who had taken over from or were about to take over from more conservative fathers. Two were in bankruptcy by 1987, two had lost their land and were custom feeding cattle for investors, and one was still farming with his father's help. Their record underlines the poor judgment of both lenders and farmers. As inflation increased, borrowing reached a crescendo and indeed in two cases persisted even after the downturn.

For all their poor business sense, however, it is important to remember that these farmers and many other Iowans like them were battling forces with which they could not compete. They were individuals attempting to succeed in a market dominated by large western feedlots that specialized in custom feeding cattle for wealthy investors in search of tax write-offs. In order to succeed in the notoriously risky cattle business, it was necessary to eliminate as much risk as possible. The western cattle men made sure investors took much of the risk, but Iowa farmers had to shoulder the risk of market fluctuations themselves. About the only strategy available to them was the use of hedging on the mercantile exchange. Unfortunately hedging required considerable knowledge, and for some it proved a double-edged weapon.

On balance, then, the repeated borrowing over these years was not an indicator of recklessness among farmers. Cattle feeding required a steady flow of borrowed capital. What these farmers and their lenders did not appreciate was the danger of structural change in their industry. That and an especially bad cyclical downturn were about to alter the financial environment of the large Iowa cattle feeder for the immediate future.[7]

The long-and short-term creditors of the sample families in the middle seventies are shown in Table 3. Certainly the most notable apsect of the data was that as many as 21 percent of the families had no long-term obligations whatever at that time. Some were to enter the land market after 1975 and would have to pay increasingly high prices; some were fortunate to have com-

Table 2. Borrowing Behavior, Five Large Cattle Feeders, Benton
County

Date	Lender	Amount of Loan
Farmer A		
1970	Land Bank	$49,200
1972	Land Bank	37,800
1974	Land Bank	126,000
1976	Citizens National Bank	23,000
1976	Citizens National Bank	41,500
1977	Land Bank	552,900
1977	Production Credit Association	300,000
1978	Small Business	54,000
1981	Metropolitan Life	120,000
1982	Production Credit Association	500,000
1984	FBS Agri-Credit	1,550,000
Farmer B		
1976	Land Bank	$81,600
1978	Production Credit Association	100,000
1979	Production Credit Association	200,000
1981	Production Credit Association	100,000
1981	Metropolitan Life	375,000
1982	Production Credit Association	400,000
1983	John Hancock	400,000
1984	Norwest Bank	580,000
Farmer C		
1975	Production Credit Association	$150,000
1977	Land Bank	637,900
1978	Small Business Administration	167,300
1979	Land Bank	652,700
1982	Metropolitan Life	1,750,000
1982	Production Credit Association	500,000
Farmer D		
1972	Land Bank	$81,600
1977	Land Bank	148,000
1981	Land Bank	293,700
1982	PCA	200,000
1983	Hancock Ins.	200,000
1984	FBS Agri-Credit	675,000
1985	FBS Agri-Credit	1,191,000
Farmer E		
1973	Metropolitan Life	$160,000
1973	Production Credit Association	200,000
1977	Metropolitan Life	350,000
1983	FBS Agri-Credit	900,000

Source: Chattel Mortgage Ledgers, County Recorder, Benton County, Vinton,
Iowa.

Table 3. Lenders to Sample Families, 1975

	Percentage of Families	Number of Families
Long-Term Lenders		
None	21	28
Federal Land Bank	43	58
Private contract	19	25
Insurance company	11	15
Bank	1	1
Farmer's Home Administration	4	5
Short-Term Lenders		
Production Credit Association	24	32
Local bank	62	83
Metropolitan bank	2	2
Self-financed	7	10
Farmer's Home Administration	6	8

Source: Sample data.
Note: Percentages may not add up to a hundred because of rounding. Three families were renters and had no long-term loans.

pleted land purchases before the boom had gathered impetus; still others never entered the land market. Among those with long-term debt, the usual source was the Federal Land Bank. After 1980, when the Land Bank instituted a variable interest rate on long-term loans, these borrowers were vulnerable. Moreover, the Land Bank created much ill-feeling when it began rating farmers according to their credit worthiness. Those who had borrowed through private contracts were generally in a better position to weather uncertain times. In these "seller mortgages" the buyer negotiated terms and interest rates directly with the seller and then made payments accordingly. Often relatives were involved in the transaction, or at least the two parties were neighbors who had known each other for many years. In any event, this was a flexible and more humanized way of buying real estate than doing business with a giant bureaucracy. Insurance companies also invested money in the land market through mortgages to farmers. Although the insurance companies were less aggressive than the Land Bank in the administration of nonperforming loans, their borrowers were nonetheless at considerable risk once the downturn came. These large operations were less likely to borrow from the Farmers' Home Administration until the late seventies, when policy changes allowed larger farmers to take advantage of disaster and guaranteed loans from FmHA. Generally, however, these were for short-term operating expenses, originally secured through local banks.

The latter dominated short-term lending for operating expenses. Farmers needed these funds to buy feed, seed, livestock, and gasoline, to make repairs, and most important of all, for living expenses. Many families simply could not obtain a steady cash flow from farm products. Grain farmers, for instance, theoretically had an annual payoff when their crop went to market. Farm program payments and grain storage tended to spread income generation throughout the year, however. Livestock farmers went to market more often, but there was a lag time of many months between the purchase of cattle by a feeder and the sale of the animals for profit. Hog farmers, especially those with continuous factorylike farrowing operations, were capable of generating a good cash flow throughout the year, and dairymen secured a milk check every two weeks. For most families, however—the exceptions were a handful of conservative farmers able to finance themselves—operating money in the form of short-term loans, renewable annually, was essential.

Local banks usually took care of a family's needs, unless a large line of operating credit was needed. In such cases families often moved over to a larger, metropolitan bank or the Production Credit Association. During the boom farmers tended to move their business from one institution to another quite often, because smaller, more conservative institutions were not capable of supporting expansion on the desired scale. In this period the Production Credit Association became very aggressive in recruiting dissatisfied customers from smaller institutions, and a number of sample families moved their portfolios in this direction.

Farmers were not the only members of a local business community to chafe at the conservative lending practices of small local banks. In Odebolt, in the sample area in northwest

Iowa, farmers and businessmen alike were so dissatisfied with the unwillingness of their bank to alter its lending philosophy that in 1979 they sought to move a neighboring bank from a nearby town to their own. They achieved their objective after a stormy meeting of the state banking commission. Six years later the transplanted bank failed.[8]

In the summer of 1985 in the middle of the farm crisis, another kind of movement of loan portfolios took place. This time financially sound farm families looking for lower interest rates on long-term loans jettisoned their connection with the Land Bank and looked to commercial institutions for their needs. Ironically, many were welcomed by small conservative banks that had refused to risk large operating loans to customers only a few years before.

The Pressures of Expansion

From the perspective of 1987, few families could take much comfort in knowing that their expansion had been a rational economic choice in the inflationary environment of the late seventies. For those with children who wanted to farm, the logic of purchasing land was even more understandable. In the seventies for the first time in their lives some farmers could live on a budget that put them on a par with the urban middle class. Therefore, it was not surprising that many parents displayed a generosity toward their children that far exceeded what they had received from their own parents. The powerful legacy of the Depression had hung over their start in farming. Then, less assistance had been available, and hard work and self-sacrifice had been the requisites of getting established. "I never dared buy anything while father was alive," exclaimed one operator. In the seventies, unfortunately, this respondent made up for lost time when his sons entered farming in a partnership. Parents were in a position to assist children who, to quote one farmer, "lived in the land of plenty," where dreams of clothes, cars, and cruises tended to distort a value system that placed hard work before the acquisition of luxuries.

Hindsight suggests that farmers who eventually found themselves in difficulty had overspent on big-ticket consumer dura-

Table 4. Expansion of Operations, 1970-1981

	Percentage of Families	Number of Families
Bought land	56	76
Constructed farm buildings	60	81
Expanded enterprise	69	93
Built or remodeled home	39	53
Helped a child begin farming	55	74

Source: Sample data.

bles and the construction of new homes. It must be remembered, however, that it was difficult for farm families to differentiate necessary expenditures for work from less essential family purchases. In previous decades farmers had often subscribed to the tradition of plowing everything back into the operation; most had been satisfied with a low standard of living. Then in the inflationary environment of the boom, eager lenders and spiraling land values combined to allow families both to live well and to expand their operations.

It would be reasonable to hypothesize that the greatest pressure for expansion would be felt by those families with sons or sons-in-law ready to begin farming in the decade of the seventies. Although not every family in the study was in this category, each had two or more family units that depended to some degree on the farm for their livelihood. Thus, as Tables 4 and 5 show, a majority increased the scale of their operations in some fashion, and as many as 39 percent remodeled or built a new home for one family unit. Did younger family members unduly influence the decision to increase the size of the operation in some way? Fully 55 percent of families made sizable material contributions to their children's start in farming—cosigned notes from the bank for purchase of land and machinery, deeded them a generous share of the partnership or corporate pie, or helped them start a herd of livestock. In most cases all the parties involved participated in the decision to purchase land (Table 5). In only 17 percent of families did fathers alone make the decision. It is

Table 5. Family Members Involved in Land Purchase Decision

	Percentage of Families	Number of Families
Head only	17	23
Both spouses	37	50
Children and parents	64	62

Source: Sample data. Respondents were asked who made the decision and were given these three choices of response.

worth noting that of this group, 60 percent bought land, and 52 percent gave some assistance to their children. Though they retained the decision for themselves, they did not refuse to expand or to support their children's careers.

Rising land prices made help from parents indispensable; without it, few children could hope to launch themselves. Rental property was increasingly hard to find, and in some instances families were forced to buy land in order to continue farming it. Hence, if the business was to remain viable in support of two or more families, it was logical to counteract inflation and rising land prices by the purchase of land and to increase the efficiency of the operation with larger machinery and livestock facilities. The timing of these decisions would eventually determine whether a farm remained strong in the middle eighties. Some families bought land before the price rose too high to pay for itself; others managed to finance purchases through private contracts at reasonable interest rates; others, however, had to wait until children came of age to farm and were forced to pay exorbitant prices and high interest rates. Land, the object of this scramble, was considered a limited resource—"they won't make any more land." Those who were interested in encouraging farmers to enter the land market were able to persuade them that land would always rise in price, that they should buy now to forestall further increases.

Only a small percentage of sample families could be described as plungers; the majority were reasonably conservative or professional in their mode of operation (Table 6). For example, 19 percent of the sample was professional in style. Over the years

Table 6. Family Style and Landownership, 1983

	Percentage of Families	Number of Families	Mean Acres Owned
Conservative	15	20	300
Middle of the road	51	68	365
Professional	19	25	617
Plunger	16	22	1,037

Sources: Sample data.
Note: Conservative denotes extreme caution in the land market and in operating style; professional denotes a style encouraged by land grant colleges, including stringent record keeping, the use of computers, leadership in farm organizations, and continual efforts to improve the farm; plunger denotes incautious expansion through leveraging and complete inattention to cash flow; middle of the road denotes diversified operations with a good balance between expansion and debt repayment.

they had upgraded their facilities, had a good understanding of marketing, kept sophisticated records; they were often leaders in farm organizations. Another 15 percent was conservative, showing extreme caution in the land market and in operating style. A further 16 percent tended to plunge into the boom economy, using leveraging as a tool of expansion in the seventies and paying little heed to the notion of cash flow. Finally, 51 percent could be classified as middle-of-the-roaders. These farmers had diversified operations and kept a balance between expansion and the payment of debts.

Every family was caught up in the boom psychology at one time or another. But, when decisions had to be made, some remained unswayed by all the excitement. As one father said to his son, "If you want to put me down in Independence [the local mental health facility] you buy that land." Another conservative father claimed that he "looked at land every day in the seventies but couldn't put a pencil to it to make it work." These farmers and others like them either rented more land if they could and purchased machinery to work it or persuaded their sons to concentrate on livestock production.

Many did take steps to calculate the kind of return expensive land would produce. If the figures were unrealistic, the matter was dropped. But the pressures for expansion were so great, the difficulties of finding rental ground always present, and the logic of buying an adjoining farm so strong, that the decision was often made regardless of rational economic expectations.

Even though the countryside was awash in credit in the middle and late seventies, the resources available to a family were important in determining how and where they expanded. Stable and reasonably affluent farm families in the community had a better chance of securing prime land in the neighborhood than the less well established. In one community a leading family was able to outbid neighbors on much of the land that came up for sale in the immediate area, assembling a compact operation piece by piece at the expense of others who wanted to control some of this land. Those who could not afford to pay over thirty-five hundred dollars an acre had to look farther afield. They looked for property in southern Iowa, southern Minnesota, northern Missouri, or even Texas. The logistics of running a farm so distant from the home place often required that one of the family move to the new farm permanently. Otherwise, the family would have to become "suitcase" farmers. One younger son in the sample who, in his father's words, "did not get into this thing to speculate," moved to newly purchased land in Missouri and demonstrated some commitment to the new locale by marrying a local girl. But most families were more inclined to treat these purchases as speculative; they planted the land in grain and enrolled it in government programs.

Age Cohorts and Selectivity

Whatever their strategies in this time of cyclical economic change, families were subject to the accident of timing, which played a strong role in determining the success or failure of their decisions.[9] The major life course transitions in agriculture—the start of a career, attainment of ownership, transfer of managerial responsibility, and full retirement—all take place against a backdrop of events outside individual control. Thus, the oldest men involved in this study—those over sixty in 1975—had started their farm careers in the depths of the Depression. Though their early years were difficult, they were able to ride the slow boom of the post–World War II years and eventually to exchange landed assets accumulated over time for those more suitable to retirement. They surrendered machinery, livestock, and some land for a retirement home in town and more liquid assets such as stocks, bonds, and certificates of deposit.

The fathers at greatest strategic risk—those aged between forty and fifty-nine in 1975—sometimes began their farm careers after military service in World War II or Korea. Some inherited land and received a worry-free start, but others had to struggle to attain ownership on their own. They experienced the full brunt of what has been termed "the agricultural treadmill."[10] These men and their wives constituted the first generation of professional managers in Iowa farming: their knowledge of agronomy, animal husbandry, and finance was far superior to that of their fathers' generation. Through the accident of timing they were in a position to plan the entry of the younger generation into farming and to work out a strategy of intergenerational transfer. It was the fate of this cohort to face the many dilemmas presented by the sudden deflation of the economy and the need to reorganize.

The sons in the sample who were under thirty in 1975 entered farming better prepared than any previous generation. Nearly half had attended college, and 20 percent had a diploma from a four-year institution. The strength of the pull of the boom was demonstrated by the fact that some sons had tried something else before coming back to farm. In fact, some members of the senior generation, ambivalent about farm careers for their children, insisted that their sons try another occupation before making the decision to farm. Some fathers tried to size up their sons' ability and their compatibility before bringing them into a close relationship. One dairyman supported his eldest son's career but would not bring him in as a partner. Instead, he waited. Later when he needed assistance in the dairy, he invited a younger son, whose temperament was more compatible, to join him. The old-style authoritarian father who made all the decisions and worked his family from morning until night was no longer common. Yet, while a more free and easy style of management was the rule, the generations were well aware that differences could develop between them. Some tried to forestall conflict by delegating responsibility. A son or brother was perhaps more comfortable with livestock, while another member of the family took charge of fieldwork, leaving the senior generation in charge of management and finance. Nevertheless, whatever the circumstances of their entry, the younger generation in this study was one of the first in history to be drawn to farming by the economic prospects created by the boom. Some families would have cause to regret their entry; as one farmer who had helped his sons begin farming in the seventies ruefully admitted ten years later, "We'd have been better off if we had never taken them in."

Some researchers found an inverse relationship between economic stress and age among all Iowa farmers. They also found a high correlation between education and size of operation and economic difficulty.[11] That is, younger and better-educated men with larger farms were more likely to get into trouble. This so-called selectivity hypothesis is less easy to test in my specialized sample of intergenerational farms. About all that can be said is that the average age of the seventy-one fathers who did not suffer economic difficulties was 63.5 years, and that of the forty-seven who did get into difficulties was 60 years, not a statistically significant result. The issue of exactly who "got into trouble," however, should wait until later.

Boom and Malaise

Farmers, agribusinessmen, and lenders were lulled into a false sense of security about the economic climate in which they were working. Some forgot many of the elementary lessons learned over the years about the need for land, buildings, and machinery to pay for themselves. When all was said and done, were the land purchases of the 1970s and early 1980s a reasonable response, or was land speculation a blunder, pursued by farmers and bankers who were "consenting adults" and who therefore had to bear responsibility for their decisions?[12]

To answer this question, it is necessary to probe more deeply into the climate of the 1970s in order to amplify the background of the boom. When respondents were asked how they would describe these years, almost to a man they remembered them as extremely satisfying. Although some mentioned problems with the weather, and others suffered livestock losses from disease, the collective memory seemed to have blotted out everything but the shock of high interest rates, something that was universally troubling. Galloping inflation and the inexorable rise in land values seemed preferable to the aftermath of the farm debt crisis and the drastic changes in agricultural finance. Yet the boom years were hardly free of stress for farm families. The cost-price squeeze, the great variability in income from year to year, the need to expand just to stay ahead of the neighbors, and the move to monoculture grain farming brought few benefits to the rural neighborhood.

If the conventional wisdom portrayed farming as all shiny four-wheel-drive tractors and "corn, beans, and Florida," there was evidence to show that agriculture during the boom had other, more troubling features. In 1978 the annual Iowa business lenders survey showed that farming had surpassed inflation as the number one "worry" among bankers. At an Iowa lenders convention that spring speakers emphasized that many farmers were having trouble paying their debts and noted that renewals of notes and refinancing were more widespread than at any time in the previous fifteen years. There were no foreclosures, but a number of voluntary sales to pay off obligations had already occurred. In some banks 10 percent of all farm customers had a cash-flow problem, and some farmers would be forced to exchange their capital-intensive operating methods for ones that were more labor intensive. Some bankers even commended the American Agriculture Movement for its protests over the cost-price squeeze.[13]

Apparently some observers intuitively felt that all was not right with the booming Iowa farm economy, and Table 7 shows that it was indeed on shaky ground throughout the seventies and early eighties. These figures represent a composite of well-managed Iowa farms statewide over the years; they are intended to give a general picture of costs and returns, rather than to illustrate the wide variation in income and assets from one farm to the next. The value of an acre of farmland doubled between 1971 and 1975, and again between 1975 and 1981. On the other hand, net farm income fluctuated from highs in the good years of 1973 and 1978 to poor years in 1976 and especially 1981. Even more telling were the so-called return-to-management figures, which

Table 7. Iowa Farm Costs and Returns, Statewide, 1971-1985

Year	Net Farm Income (Cash)	Management Return	Land Value per Acre	Total Assets*
1971	$14,995	$ 396	$ 410	$178,490
1972	29,162	11,943	500	224,591
1973	54,226	30,394	555	262,118
1974	29,497	2,757	658	308,387
1975	33,135	5,799	843	359,915
1976	26,108	− 6,352	1,004	476,382
1977	29,606	− 4,824	1,106	520,450
1978	56,555	20,146	1,208	575,813
1979	44,642	− 2,014	1,332	650,298
1980	52,206	− 171	1,537	748,483
1981	21,944	− 18,450	1,603	766,879
1982	29,508	− 12,430	1,626	767,088
1983	23,883	− 14,261	1,471	755,277
1984	27,312	− 19,372	1,425	439,049
1985	31,544	− 10,220	1,227	384,207

Source: Cooperative Extension Service, Iowa State University, *Iowa Farm Costs and Returns* (Ames, 1972-86).
*The 1984 and 1985 total assets included owned assets only. Before 1984, rented assets were calculated in this total.

measure net farm income less 6 percent interest on net worth and the wages of the operator and his family. Obviously in both 1973 (after the grain deal) and 1978 many farmers made money, but losses occurred in 1976 and 1977 and every year after 1979. The first five years of the eighties were a disaster. These figures demonstrate the fragility of the Iowa farm economy, and the lack of foundation for the optimism reflected in higher living standards and urban-patterned life-styles.

An Iowa poll of 432 farm families conducted in the spring of 1979 is worth analyzing at some length, for it brings out the general malaise and ambivalence with which farmers viewed their situation at the height of the boom. The poll, among other things, probed changing life-styles, political opinions, attitudes toward government involvement in agriculture, and ecological questions.

Overall, farmers were creatures of contradiction and self-interest. They said, for example, that they would pay no more than fifteen hundred dollars for an acre of land, but they were not prepared to sell for less than two thousand dollars. From 1972 to 1978 farmland in Iowa had increased in value by 24 percent, but 60 percent of respondents said they had been harmed by inflation, and only 26 percent claimed to have been helped. At the same time, 66 percent said they were better off in 1979 than they had been ten years before. Some gave insights into what these contradictions meant. An older farmer, who had rented out or sold much of his land, remarked that "personally inflation helped. I was quite a plunger, the times made me what I am, at the expense of others. The man that tills the soil, that's the man who is being hurt today." The high cost of farm inputs and low commodity prices appeared to be the stumbling blocks. A younger farmer emphasized this point. "What good is land," he asked, "unless you are going to sell it? It looks good on paper, but to operate you have to be a millionaire."[14]

In 1978 one in five Iowa farm families made a bid on farmland. But larger farmers—those owning more than 380 acres—were in the land market more often. Even though farmers were concerned about the effects of chemicals, they were more concerned that they could not farm without them. Finally, they uttered a chorus of complaints about government involvement in agriculture. Most wanted a free market. Yet there was strong sentiment for government action to cut meat imports and to raise the price of corn. One-third of farmers agreed with the contention that they would be better off if they liquidated their operations and moved to town, but they wanted their own children to farm. This ambivalence was best summed up by a young respondent, an organizer for the American Agriculture Movement who had himself felt resistance to activism designed to make things better. "Farmers," he noted, "want one thing, but yet they don't want it."[15]

The view that rampant inflation was a disaster to the countryside in the late seventies and early eighties is confirmed by the records of bankruptcy court, which provide the opportunity

Table 8. Lender Losses in Farm Bankruptcies, Iowa,
1984-1986.

Lender	Average Liability	Number of Debtors	Percentage of Sample
Land Bank	$267,980	113	38
Production Credit Association	293,409	45	15
Farmers' Home Administration	174,584	119	40
Banks	229,987	128	43
Private individuals	162,749	54	18
Insurance companies	278,047	27	9
Unsecured debt	61,109	75	25
Commodity Credit Corporation	173,202	24	8

Source: Case Files, (N = 298), Federal Bankruptcy Court, Northern and
Southern Districts of Iowa, Cedar Rapids and Des Moines.

for an extended view of economic behavior over a long period. In
most cases, bankruptcy occurs several years after the decision to
expand. There is usually an extensive lag between the closing of
a loan and the time when it is called in because of nonperfor-
mance. Federal bankruptcy files from the northern and southern
districts of Iowa for 1984-1986 contain the wreckage of thousands of decisions made by farmers and bankers in the boom
eight or ten years before. As Tables 8 and 9 indicate, the devasta-
tion was immense.

The average debt was well over half a million dollars, with
debt-to-asset ratios of 182 percent at the time of bankruptcy. (The
average farm in Iowa in 1985 had liabilities of $166,394, and a
debt-to-asset ratio of 42 percent.) In addition one-fourth of these
bankruptcies had an average of $61,109 in completely unsecured
debt, nearly all of it at elevators, feed stores, and other community institutions, which presumably had given farmers credit because they trusted their judgment and believed that the booming
economy would ensure repayment. Similarly, 43 percent of
bankrupt farmers owed money to banks, most of which were
local country institutions where the farmer was well known and
where even in the most inflationary climate some attention was
given to the client's ability to pay back the loan. For although a

Table 9. Debtor Liability in Farm Bankruptcies, Iowa,
1984-1986

	Average Debt	Average Assets	Debt-to Asset Ratio
All farmers	$ 592,365	23,797	182
Chapter 11	1,939,648	619,085	167
Young farmers	420,793	185,613	226

Source: Case Files (N = 298), Federal Bankruptcy Court, Northern and Southern Districts of Iowa, Cedar Rapids and Des Moines.

certain proportion of these cases did make unrealistic demands—one spectacular bankruptcy involved a farm family
with interests in a veterinary supply store and a beauty salon,
which handed a loss of several million dollars to various lenders—31 percent of these cases involved younger men who had
entered farming in the seventies. The liabilities of the Farmers'
Home Administration attest to the desires of those who lacked a
firm financial base to begin farming and those who utilized
disaster loans to try to reestablish themselves.

Typically the bankrupt held both short-and long-term debt.
The purchase of a quarter section, machinery, and loans for
operating expenses, were hardly extravagant in their scope. By
and large, transactions were based on the desire of the borrower
to support a family by farming. Obviously both lenders and
borrowers had expected inflation to continue. In the environment of the times their behavior could hardly be classified as
speculative.

A search to place blame, then, becomes a futile exercise.
Farmers were consenting adults, but so were bankers. The government was a major player throughout the period, and the rest
of the country also took part in the inflationary bonanza that
characterized the seventies. Perhaps what was more important
in the long term was that the downturn, when it came, was
selective. Only certain families suffered major disruption. Many
who had not changed their style of operation were hardly incon-
venienced at all. Corn-belt agriculture, as many of these farmers
remembered, tends to reward the patient.

3

Storm over the Country

Financial stress came to the families in this study in a number of ways. Usually they were unable to keep up with interest payments on land, machinery, or improvements. After a period of delinquency the lender would call in the loan, and the farmer would receive notice of a writ of replevin for the recovery of movable property or foreclosure in the case of real estate. Here, the use of the vernacular term "getting into trouble" signifies some kind of reorganization of a family farm: a negotiated or forced loss of property through give back, buy back, foreclosure, some kind of litigation in the civil court, or the filing of bankruptcy by the farm family. Any of these had a swift impact on the family, and financial difficulties inevitably created stress that made family members vulnerable to a host of other problems.

Those who were threatened with or actually suffered loss went through a cycle of reactions. Distressed family members were prone to prolonged periods of anger and depression, which sometimes resulted in suicide, alcoholism, and violent behavior.[1] As the farm crisis progressed through its own chronology over a four-year period, the circumstances surrounding financial loss and the tools available to meet it changed. By the spring of 1987, mobilization of resources at the state and local levels gave financially pressed families a far greater range of options than they had had in the fall of 1983.

But for all the trappings of mobilization, one factor remained more or less constant: such was the stigma surrounding failure that families often sought help too late to save themselves. As a farmer who had fought foreclosure by the Land Bank for over a year expressed it, "It's a sad situation with farm people; if things get tough, everyone clams up." There was no great show of solidarity among farmers. Ashamed of failure, most worked hard to deny what was happening, and families in trouble had to fend for themselves.[2] Thus, the proverbial independence of farmers held sway even in the face of catastrophe. Because of this behavior pattern, the circumstances under which economic stress occurred were more trying in 1983-1985, than they were two years later.

It is important to keep in mind the sensitive nature of the subject matter in this chapter. Of the fifty-eight sample families that suffered setbacks in the farm crisis, many were interviewed months if not years after the most dramatic events in their fall had taken place. However, such was the slow pace of the resolution of their problems that contact with lenders, lawyers, and creditors continually reminded them of past experience and prevented them from finally putting this stage of their lives behind them. It was obvious that some respondents were still greatly affected by their experience, but it was inappropriate to attempt to gauge the depth of psychological trauma in a relatively short formal interview designed to elicit a wide range of data. Therefore, such sensitive issues as the incidence of alcoholism, violence, and depression were avoided in order to concentrate on the chronological and factual aspects of the respondents' experiences in the previous decade.

Finally, it is important to emphasize that until victims of the farm crisis were confronted face-to-face, it was impossible to comprehend the magnitude of their experience. In view of the vast sums of money spent on farm programs, the media exposure, and the variety of social programs designed to assist those in difficulties, together with the selectivity of the downturn, there is a temptation to treat the farm crisis with a degree of cynicism as a "pseudo crisis." Just a few minutes of conversation with a family that had gone through the mill of the farm downturn quickly dispels such a view.

Who Got into Trouble

I was interested in finding out what possible combination of factors best predicted economic difficulty for the 135 families in the sample. The data from the interviews were coded, and correlations were run with various combinations of variables included in the analysis. I ran a stepwise regression with fourteen independent variables and the variable Trouble as the dependent. Trouble was measured 1 if the family had suffered bankruptcy, foreclosure, had had to renegotiate with a lender, or had given back land because of failure to make payments. Otherwise, Trouble was coded 0. In addition, most of the independent variables were measured dichotomously. Thus, those who had a long-term mortgage were coded 1 and those who did not, 0. The independent variables included inheritance, the age of the father, the age of the son, the style of operation, whether the family bought land, the short-term lender, the long-term lender, the education of the son, acres owned, acres rented, whether the family changed lenders, the organization of the business, the type of operation, and the number of families involved in an operation.

Only four variables were statistically significant at the .05 level. Expansion, receiving no inheritance, changing a lender, and having a long-term debt—in that order—proved the most powerful predictors of failure, explaining 33 percent of the variance in the following equation (standard errors are in parentheses):

$$\text{Trouble} = .018 + .306 \text{ Expan} - .285 \text{ Inher} +$$
$$(.080) \qquad (.075)$$
$$.189 \text{ Changelend} + .26 \text{ Lendlo}$$
$$(.080) \qquad\qquad (.091)$$
$$\text{R Square} = .33; \text{N} = 135$$

On the face of it, the only predictor that might not have been anticipated is inheritance. That economic difficulties related to the farm crisis came to those not fortunate to receive assistance in their farm careers through inheritance was an important finding. I will explore it at some length later.

To take this analysis a shade further and make the results more interpretable, I performed a multiple classification analysis on the data. The four significant variables had the results displayed in Table 10. If a family inherited property it had 28 percent less chance of getting into economic difficulties than if it did not inherit. Changing lenders gave a family 25 percent more probability of encountering a financial setback than not chang-

Table 10. Multiple Classification Analysis of Economic Stress

Grand Mean = .40				
	Number of Families	Adjusted Deviation from Mean	Beta	p
No inheritance	57	57	.29	.001
Inheritance	78	29		
No lender change	87	31	.25	.01
Change lender	48	56		
Independent style	49	34	.10	.22
Integrated style	86	43		
Did not buy land	59	35	.09	.32
Bought land	76	44		
Did not expand	42	26	.20	.02
Expanded	93	46		
No long-term loan	29	23	.19	.02
Long-term loan	106	45		
R squared = .30				

Source: Sample data.

ing. Expansion and long-term borrowing had a slightly smaller impact.

Thus, in trying to answer the question of who suffered financial stress in this group of farm families, standard demographic predictors such as age and education did not much affect the issue. Rather, behavior in the boom, together with the accident of inheritance, predicted how families would fare in a severe economic downturn.

Some further results, not formally displayed here, showed that the most stable enterprises were hog/dairy farms. Surprisingly, the most likely to get into trouble were dairies, although none in my sample participated in the buy-out program. They were followed by cattle feeders, cattle and hog operators, grain farmers, and finally hog farmers. Farmers' Home Administration borrowers were the most vulnerable of those with long-term obligations, followed by those indebted to the Land Bank, insurance companies, and then private contract holders.

Farm Trouble

By 1983, after four bad years, even the promise of the payment-in-kind program did not disperse the gloom hovering over Iowa agriculture. In small communities around the state many people were strategically placed to comprehend the seriousness of the situation. The economy was overburdened with debt. Routine business was largely run on credit, and the monthly "blue credit sheets" that circulated to subscribers clearly indicated which farmers were beginning to feel the pinch. But though a close watch was kept on this kind of intelligence, silence and denial were the rule among farmers and businessmen alike. Some farmers as well as agribusiness people were privy to the details of the credit picture. As members of the boards of elevators, cooperatives, the Land Bank, and the Farmers' Home Administration, they saw information that caused them concern not only for their relatives, friends, and neighbors but sometimes for themselves as well. One farmer moved his business from one local bank to another after a stint on the county Farmers' Home Administration board made him aware of certain management practices at his original bank. About a year later both banks collapsed under the weight of agricultural losses. Another farmer had a board membership on one of the most plunger-oriented Land Banks in Iowa. His tenure was made doubly difficult because his own highly leveraged position corresponded closely to that of many of the institution's members who were in the process of being liquidated. They at least had the option of seeking protection from their lenders through bankruptcy, but his board position made it hard to maneuver without raising the issue of conflict of interest. In the end he retained his position and surrendered his land without a fight.

The years 1983-1984 were a time when farmers in economic difficulties were mostly alone in their fight to save themselves. Their options were limited. They could try to sell some of their assets; they could attempt to negotiate and refinance with their lender; or they could contemplate bankruptcy, especially Chapter 11 reorganization. All these alternatives were complex and called for the assistance of a lawyer knowledgeable about arcane agriultural law and the intricacies of refinancing. Lawyers and accountants had become very efficient in the seventies at assisting farmers with the problems associated with an inflationary economy, but not surprisingly many were ignorant of the strategies required for passage through a deflationary climate. In essence this was a period of learning for farmers, lenders and attorneys, when costly mistakes were made by all parties because of their unfamiliarity with the situation in which they found themselves.

In these early days such was the stigma attached to bankruptcy that some, under the illusion that the lender was their "partner and friend," made little effort to protect themselves. The trusting relationship they had taken for granted evaporated, however, once lenders had to choose between the institution that employed them and the welfare of the farmer-borrowers. It was the period of the "horror story," when lenders scrambled to recoup steadily mounting losses in any fashion. Negotiations that farmers began in good faith would rapidly take a different turn. Credit was cut off, judgments were served for nonpayment of loans, and writs of replevin were issued to enable lenders to repossess livestock and machinery. This alteration in the lender-borrower relationship usually came with shocking suddenness and was often accompanied by harassment and questionable business practices designed to pressure the client into submission. Some lenders hired so-called hatchet men, who, because they had no ties with the community, could perform the necessary housecleaning chores with a minimum of restraint.

For a number of the early failures in the sample there was an element of luck in which direction they turned initially. One farmer of a large operation in northwest Iowa was able to have his Chapter 11 bankruptcy plan approved by the Farm Credit System. Shortly afterward the policy was changed, and the Farm Credit System refused to cooperate with bankruptcy reorganization plans. In northeast Iowa a local bank tried to repossess property from a large dairy. The father and son decided to ignore the stigma their community attached to suing a "respected" institution and filed a lawsuit against the bank. Fortunately for the family, the institution had made a number of mistakes in its haste to secure assets, and the lawsuit saved part of their operation. Shortly thereafter, however, the son left Iowa for a position in the Central Valley of California.

Like these casualties, several of those who failed early were those with larger farms who had aggressively expanded in the seventies and whose considerable assets were tempting plums for banks frantic to recoup their losses. Although the numbers are too small to make statistically valid generalizations, to a man the half dozen upper-class operators in the sample who failed got into trouble in 1983, and all followed the route of negotiation rather than litigation with lenders. They did so because they believed at the time that it was the way a businessman should behave. They were often the social equals of the lenders, and their upbringing required them to maintain a polite and businesslike exterior even under the most stressful conditions. Thus, with legal counsel they attempted to negotiate their way out of difficulties. Such a strategy might have been promising in more prosperous times, but with the economy on the downturn, they found that lenders took advantage of their situation. Four years later these families were still bitter about the conduct of their lenders, and pointed to their own trusting behavior as a major cause of their problems. Nevertheless, whatever strategy these early casualties followed, the odds were that it would be doomed to failure because of the deterioration of the economy throughout 1984-1985.

Even as upper-class farmers were trusting their bankers, some ordinary dirt farmers had dismissed the stigma attached to bankruptcy and had begun visiting their attorneys' offices to embrace the protection of Chapter 11. The Chapter 11 bankruptcy, designed as it was for commercial firms, was a blunt instrument with which to guide a farm through difficult economic times. While it did allow for reorganization and prevented a creditor from seizing assets, it possessed a major disadvantage: like any reorganization plan designed to pay off debts, it was drawn up with relatively optimistic expectations. Chapter 11 plans assumed that prices for commodities would remain at a certain level. Unfortunately they continued down a precipitous slope. Moreover, many Chapter 11s were not approved, partly because lenders would not agree to the terms of reorganization or judges considered them unworkable. In essence, then, Chapter 11 became a form of holding action—in some cases a desperate last-ditch effort—whereby farmers tried to wait out the storm. Often they were forced to take out a full bankruptcy (a Chapter 7), under which all property was liquidated to pay debts. Others survived until the economy improved in the second half of 1986, and they were able to negotiate with their creditors under the auspices of the state mediation program.

In 1983-1984 the economic climate did not encourage negotiation, and responses to lender intransigence were few. In some communities those who found themselves in difficulties developed a kind of underground network of farmer advocacy. Attorneys were not of much help, partly because local lawyers had little knowledge of bankruptcy law and because they were reluctant to fight the local establishment for the rights of farmers. A few farmers, therefore, acted *pro se* (literally, for oneself) in order to protect themselves. Self-taught in agricultural law, these men became experts in some of its more arcane aspects in order to block lenders bent on repossessing land, machinery, or livestock. They researched old statutes, used the federal rather than state courts to improve their chances of success, and sometimes succeeded in fighting their lender adversaries to a standstill. Bankers, not surprisingly, railed against these self-styled experts. In some cases this *pro se* activity was encouraged by right-wing extremists whose itinerant messengers saw an opportunity to stir up hatred among vulnerable farmers.[3] But whatever the origins of this militancy, the actions of the farm families involved were symptomatic of the atmosphere of the "confrontation" period of the farm crisis.

Some sample members went through several stages of reorganization. They took out Chapter 11, then filed for a Chapter 7; they gave back part of their property to placate creditors, then lost everything soon after through foreclosure. Whatever the pattern, Tables 11 and 12 describe their experiences and the timing of their actions as nearly as possible. Of the 135 sample families, 58 encountered trouble and had to reorganize in some

Table 11. Reorganization Strategies of Farm Families in Trouble

Strategy	Percentage Adopting	Number Adopting
Bankruptcy	19	11
Giving back property	16	9
Renegotiation	34	20
Foreclosure	31	18

Source: Sample data.

Table 12. Timing of Reorganization Strategies

Date	Percentage Adopting Strategy	Number Adopting Strategy
Before 1985	34	20
1985	29	17
1986	24	14
1987	12	7

Source: Sample data.

fashion. A handful of prominent families, as noted, tried to negotiate. For the remainder of those in trouble, there was no clear pattern of behavior. A family was just as likely to suffer foreclosure in 1985 and 1986. The new agricultural Chapter 12 bankruptcy was introduced in the fall of 1986, but inasmuch as only two sample cases were handled under Chapter 12, most of the bankruptcies took place before then. The randomness of the actions in some ways reflect the dispersal of cases over these years. About a third occurred before 1985, with a roughly equal representation in the other two years. The establishment of the mediation program in 1986 tended to boost the renegotiation totals. Nevertheless it is intriguing to note that if bankruptcy and foreclosure are seen as indicators of "fight" by the farm family and give-back and negotiation as signs of relative "passivity," the incidence of both was exactly equal.

What was the initial reaction of a family suddenly confronted with the reality of lender pressure? By early 1984 the

Iowa Farm Unity Coalition hotline in Des Moines was becoming
a well-used resource. As advocates the counselors gave callers
concrete information about their rights in foreclosure, bankruptcy, and repossession proceedings, as well as the names of
attorneys willing to take on farm cases. This resource and, after
February 1985, the state's own hotline, were one possible first
step toward bringing order to a farm family's sudden chaotic
situation. Obviously, families learned about alternative strategies in many ways. Relatives, friends, local farm advocates,
attorneys, the Cooperative Extension Service (if the agent was
deemed sympathetic and had some rapport with the community), and the clergy were just some of the resource people available to give useful advice and a sympathetic ear. By the fall of
1984 community farm crisis committees were springing up all
over Iowa, and that winter public meetings became a common
arena in which to glean information.

In view of the complexity of the situation in which many
families found themselves, perhaps it is not surprising that
many behaved in ways that made a successful outcome to their
problems difficult. The so-called do-nothing syndrome remained common throughout the farm crisis. Farmers had great
inertia to overcome if they were to combat the forces arrayed
against them. Yet at a time when families needed to be at their
most innovative and alert, community and business loyalties,
the stigma of failure, and the numbing shock of what was happening tended to bring on a state of paralysis.[4] In effect, each
family that got into trouble had to reinvent the wheel.

One example of the pattern should suffice. On one grain
farm, a closely held family corporation, a father and his two sons
worked as full-time operators. The parents seemed oblivious to
the dangerous situation they were in, even taking a vacation in
the early spring of 1985. When they returned they were summoned to the Production Credit Association office and told they
would no longer receive operating funds. As often happened, the
family was galvanized from total passivity into a veritable flurry
of activity once the full realization of the situation sank in. By the
early summer this family had put their house and much of their
land up for sale, had filed for Chapter 11, and had seen their sons
leave for off-farm work elsewhere. There were no buyers, how-

ever, and the parents settled down to a limbolike existence for the next two years. Their Chapter 11 plan was never approved, but they were able to take advantage of farm programs and so hang on through another two planting seasons, using their deficiency payments and the goodwill of the local elevator to farm after a fashion.

Certainly the most dramatic and tragic manifestation of the farm crisis was the incidence of suicide, the ultimate symptom of familial and societal inability to come to grips with the special problems involved in farm failure. From 1980 to 1985 281 farmers committed suicide in Iowa, an average of 47 each year. At least in Iowa the number of suicides did not increase after 1983. Indeed, there were four fewer farmer suicides in 1984 than in 1980. In other states of the upper Midwest—Wisconsin, Minnesota, and the Dakotas, for example—farmer suicides sharply increased through the period. The explanation for the flat trajectory of the Iowa figures must rest with the very successful mobilization of private and then state agencies to channel farmers toward constructive ways of solving their problems. At the same time, the farmer suicide rate in Iowa was high throughout these years—about twice that of urban adult men—and especially high for men over fifty five. In the four sample counties eighteen farmers took their lives between 1980 and 1985. Unfortunately it is impossible to tell whether these deaths were attributable to financial problems brought on by the farm crisis or to illness, alcoholism, injury, or family problems.[5]

There were two suicides involving families in this study, each a direct result of financial difficulties. The first occurred relatively early in the farm crisis, and therefore was partly due to the lack of intervention available. The other occurred in the third winter of the downturn.

In the first case, severe financial problems were beginning to surface at a hog/dairy enterprise where a father and his son toiled in partnership by 1982. The bank demanded some changes in the operation and threatened foreclosure. The next year it carried through on its threat, and despite a Chapter 11 bankruptcy, the situation continued to deteriorate. Some of the livestock were lost to disease. Then the lawyer administering the bankruptcy behaved incompetently, on more than one occasion even colluding with the bank. The parents, because of pride, were unwilling to divulge their true situation to their children, either on or off the farm. By the fall of 1983 there was little available cash to feed the livestock and to provide basic necessities for the family. To save money the family turned off the heat and returned Christmas presents to stores for cash. The father began walking between farms to do chores. In the spring of 1984 the bank continued to harass the farmer, making telephone calls at all hours of the day and evening and sending officers out unannounced to check on inventory. The farmer, able to envision no respite from this grim situation, fell into a deep depression from which he never recovered. In July 1984 his son found him hanging in the barn.

The circumstances of this tragedy illustrate two phenomena that were fairly common in the early stages of the farm crisis. Lenders were ruthless in pursuit of farmers' assets, showing little understanding of the consequences their polices might bring, and families in desperate straits, particularly if the family head was over fifty, did everything possible to hide their difficulties not only from the community but even from close relatives. In fact this very suicide did a great deal to alert others to the dangers of isolation, for it received a good deal of national publicity in the winter of 1984-1985. Local communities, church congregations, and families learned to watch for the danger signals that precede suicide.

Nevertheless, even widespread knowledge of the problem and thorough integration into a community could not prevent suicide in some instances. In the second case in my sample a family lived with an eighty-year-old mother from whom they were buying land on contract. The failure to secure a Farmers' Home Administration loan in 1985 prevented them from cementing a deteriorating relationship with their local bank. In the fall the farmer got involved with a Chicago farm-consulting firm, which, for a hefty up-front fee, guaranteed to solve the family's financial problems. At an interview shortly after this contact was made, the father expressed profound relief that he had stumbled across the consultant's advertisement in a farm paper, and he seemed optimistic that this assistance would extract the family

Table 13. Actions of Farmers in Financial Trouble, 1983-1987

	Percentage	Number
Attended crisis meetings	60	32
Became an activist	22	13
Cooperated with lender	48	27
Counseled other farmers	52	30
Sold or gave back land	55	32
Eliminated enterprise	50	29
Sold machinery	35	20
Took off-farm job	36	21

Source: Sample data (N = 58).

from its financial quagmire. Evidently this optimism was short-lived, for he took his own life that winter.

Immediate Reactions to Trouble

The figures in Table 13 illustrate the reluctance or the inability of those in trouble to organize for protest or constructive response. Only 60 percent ever attended a crisis meeting of any kind, and even fewer counseled other farmers in trouble. The lack of effective leadership was especially notable among prominent farmers whose actions early in the farm crisis might perhaps have alerted others to what was happening and forestalled the worst effects. One such farmer explained his attitude, "Any outspokenness on my part would have jeopardized my situation, and therefore I kept quiet." Most were not only afraid of doing anything lenders might see in a bad light but also extremely reluctant to admit their financial difficulties to their neighbors. Indeed, when sample families were asked how they managed to survive the first weeks and months of travail, 96 percent of them said they had relied on "individual coping." In addition, 72 percent said that their religious faith gave them comfort. At least initially, all but a few tried to go it alone. They were reluctant to share their difficulties with others.

But it would be wrong to give the impression that all families stoically endured by themselves. I attended one old-fashioned neighborhood get-together in northeast Iowa in March of 1985. The host had already lost his livestock to the bank, but in a defiant gesture he had held back one pig for a roast. While the children played basketball, neighbors and friends sat around the living room swapping "horror stories." When it was time to eat, the pig was carved and the visitors crowded into the kitchen for a huge meal of roast pork with all the trappings. Others stopped by after lunch to express their support to a family in the first stages of losing their farm.

The farm crisis gave some the opportunity for activism in the area of financial and legal counseling. In the sample as a whole, thirteen families could be classified as activists in the sense that they had often counseled other families, had organized farm crisis committees, or had spoken at crisis meetings. One of the best routes to expertise in agricultural law and finance was experience. Therefore, most activists came from the ranks of farmers involved in foreclosure, bankruptcy, or some other fight with a lender over assets. Often the activist member of the family was the wife. She did not carry around the guilt that accompanied failure, often had fewer inhibitions than her husband about activism, and was usually better at organizing and networking.

Such was the case with the wife of one dairyman. Her crusade for farmers' rights took her all over Iowa on speaking engagements. She organized protests and meetings and traveled to Washington to lobby at the headquarters of the Farmers' Home Administration. Her family had not had the resources to bring a son into partnership; so he had begun on his own with the assistance of a Land Bank loan. Unfortunately, a series of droughts in the early eighties devastated his crops, and the Land Bank initiated foreclosure proceedings. It was then that the parents learned that they had unintentionally cosigned for their son's land. The vice-president for credit at the local Land Bank waved a foreclosure notice in their faces. "There's just no sense your going on," he said; "we aren't just talking about your son's land; we're talking about yours also, because you cosigned his loan papers." It was at that moment that the wife realized what she was up against. From then on she relied on her own dictum, "In

God we trust; in all others we have it in writing.'"6 This woman's outspoken advocacy on behalf of farmer's rights proved that protest could pay dividends, that "the squeaky wheel gets the grease." In her case activism saved her farm and others for another few years. Moreover, her campaign against the Farmers' Home Administration eventually brought improved service for others.

One of the basic strategies of lenders during the years 1983-1985 was to satisfy the bank examiners by forcing farmers to relinquish assets so the institution's portfolio would show some improvement. At first they were reasonably successful in this shortsighted policy, but it would prove unfortunate in the long term. Ruthless pursuit of assets only alienated the farm population and made it difficult to do business with farmers once the worst of the downturn passed. Over half the sample members who got into difficulties either sold or gave back land. Either alternative had an immediate negative psychological impact on the farmer, but it could be materially beneficial to some extent. The family no longer had to make expensive loan payments or to pay taxes on the relinquished property. At the same time many misunderstood their liability in surrendering land. Farmers were often required to furnish a deficiency payment to the lender (i.e., the difference between the selling price and the amount of the original loan), and there were complex tax implications also. Thus, many were forced into Chapter 11 even after disposing of land, for in bankruptcy these tax and deficiency questions were left unanswered for the duration. In broad terms, the flooding of the land market only tended to depress prices and inhibit sales. Some families, at the urging of lenders, attempted to sell land in 1983, only to find that buyers had disappeared from the market.

Far more unfortunate from the viewpoint of the individual farm family was the insistence of the lender that the family sell income-producing property—i.e., livestock and machinery. Many farms had too much machinery in any case, but putting so much on the market at one time forced prices down and destroyed the market for new machinery. The sale of livestock, especially breeding stock, and the refusal to finance cattle and feeder pig purchases disrupted the cash flow of an operation just

at the time when cash availability rather than equity had become
a basis for judging financial soundness.

If the livestock enterprise was eliminated, as it was in twen-
ty-nine of the fifty-eight financially troubled farms, income-
producing capacity was jeopardized. Apart from government
farm payments, there was little left with which to generate income to save the farm. Unfortunately, far too many farmers
cooperated with their lenders in reorganization. At least 48
percent followed the dictates of their "friendly" banker, only to
discover that they had been misled. A number of farm families
eliminated an enterprise or sold machinery as a condition of
receiving crop financing for the following year and then, a short
time later, faced foreclosure. Yet, in truth, lenders were often as
confused as farmers in their search to act responsibly in a sharply changing economy. According to a farmer with considerable
financial acumen, his local bank "couldn't decide what to do" in
the winter of 1985-1986 when he supplied it with a good set of
records on his operation. For four months they dithered about
whether to fund him for another year. In the end he went elsewhere. Too often the desire to stem the tide of red ink overnight
caused lenders to cut off the hand that fed them with interest
payments.

Another strategy urged on farmers was off-farm employment
for one or more members of the family. These jobs will receive
greater attention later, but it is important to note now that only a
handful of families who suffered followed the formula that the
agricultural establishment advocated: to leave farming altogether and change careers. Successful career change required a
mindset that considered an alternative occupation an opportunity, and a chance to avoid the huge amount of stress entailed in
staying on the farm.

One northwest Iowa family can serve as an example. In 1985
the father-son operation was floundering, and rather than face
what looked like an inevitable failure, they resolved to leave
farming altogether. The son and his wife, who was a nurse,
moved to Arizona and obtained employment in a laboratory and
a hospital, respectively. Meanwhile the parents concentrated on
dealing with the Land Bank. Considering that 1985 was not a
good year for negotiations, their attitude presumably had some-

thing to do with the eventual agreement they signed. The father, who had worked in electronics in California in the fifties, answered an advertisement for a computer repairman and managed to obtain a job. Although his territory was some distance away, and he spent many days on the road, he and his wife were able to keep their century-old farm homestead and a few surrounding acres.

Another couple saved their acreage by setting themselves up in a windshield repair business. For them, leaving farming was the termination of a nightmare situation of endless stress, and the decision had a rejuvenating and energizing effect.

It was not possible to follow ex-farmers to other localities. Some sample families had children who had once worked on the farm and then found employment out of state. Those who had left full-time or part-time farming usually continued to live on their farm acreage. Of the 135 families, 36 percent had members working either full-or part-time off their farm. The wives were the obvious candidates, and some did obtain good jobs. One wife, who had finished college, became a stockbroker in a large office in Cedar Rapids. Others went back to teaching. Most, however, were engaged in minimum-wage employment wherever it was available.

Two points are worth emphasizing from this initial foray into the world of the farm family under pressure in the downturn. The evidence suggests that those who did not inherit property, especially land, tended to get into trouble in the farm crisis. This pattern says something about the structure of agriculture and the fact that by the seventies Iowa landownership was controlled by families who owed their position to family contacts. At the same time the evidence suggests that ownership of large amounts of land did not immunize a family against the farm crisis. On the contrary, large farmers were often just as dependent on borrowed capital for real estate and operating loans. Hence, those who owned more than four hundred acres had an equal chance of surviving or failing. Small farms that did not borrow for expansion were less likely to fail.[7] In short, expansion was the key factor in a failure of an operation.

The other important finding concerns the ambivalence of farm families to make aggressive attempts to save themselves, to seek alternatives once they were in trouble. Ironically, a "do nothing" strategy, though seemingly ill-conceived in the short run, proved partially correct in the long term. As the farm program took effect and resources were mobilized to assist farmers at the state level, possibilities for the recycling of a farm career grew better.

Unfortunately for some, the wait for better times seemed interminable. They often existed for months, if not years, in a state of limbo, supported by the farm program and any other resources they could lay their hands on, waiting for the farm crisis to unravel.

4

Mobilization

The farm crisis made it necessary for state, local, and private organizations to mobilize their resources to assist a traditionally independent segment of the Iowa population, accustomed to taking care of its own affairs. This time individual effort was not enough, and after February 1985 government and the private sector made an unprecedented attempt to meet the physical, legal, spiritual, and psychological needs of farmers and their families

Characteristically, though, farm families continued to act alone, even when their livelihood was threatened. They generally remained suspicious of outside assistance, spurning officially sponsored programs except in dire emergency. Often well-intentioned outsiders encountered what they perceived as indifference among farmers. Food stamp sign-up drives, mental health center open houses, and local farm crisis meetings were invariably poorly attended, partly because those suffering from the crisis were reluctant to show their neediness in front of their neighbors and partly because a good proportion of families in any area were not affected by the crisis at all.

The Battle over Hearts and Minds

One of the most intriguing aspects of the years 1983-1987 in Iowa was the rivalry between the neopopulist, profarmer activist groups and the mainstream farm organizations. For years the Farm Bureau had represented farmers at the state and national level; now its hegemony was challenged.

Neopopulism in agriculture stood for raising the level of price supports and for mandatory controls of production. In broad terms neopopulists were dedicated to tipping the balance of power toward average citizens, changing the government policies in favor of common sense and common men and women, and securing economic opportunities for all.[1] Not surprisingly neopopulists attributed the downturn in part to the sorry state of agriculture in the eighties. Farm families were in difficulties because their priorities were confused. They had relied on the gospel of agribusiness, which had pushed unsound farming practices and the expansion of debt levels as standard operating procedures. Neopopulists considered the crisis an opportunity for the regeneration of agriculture and especially the concept of the family farm.

The establishment—the Farm Bureau, the Cooperative Extension Service, the commodity organization, the state agricultural bureaucracy, and large agribusiness firms—on the other hand, had received a blow to their credibility during these years. They had, after all, encouraged big farming, and their ideas were found wanting.

The battle between these competing interests for the hearts and minds of Iowa farmers and their families revolved around the ultimate lifeline of these years: government commodity programs. While most agreed that these programs were wasteful and unfairly distributed, ultimately it was the huge infusion of funds for deficiency payments, acreage set-aside programs, dairy buyouts, and guaranteed loans that allowed many families to survive. The farm program safety net was so seductive that it largely neutralized any initiative among farmers to alter their approach to farming in the short term. Thus, while the farm crisis provided the opportunity to give serious thought to the problems of agriculture, a rigorous debate among ordinary farmers never materialized. The agricultural establishment, though damaged in 1985, was able to regroup its forces. Two years later it had recovered sufficient poise and credibility to retain its dominance as spokesman for the rank and file, principally because of its agribusiness and political connections at the state and local level. This outcome was not altogether surprising, given the fairly conservative political opinions of farmers. Moreover, by the 1980s only a fairly select group of full-time operators remained. Overwhelmingly they subscribed to the agribusiness philosophy despite the shocks many of them had sustained.

Neopopulism in Action

The principal force for change in agriculture in the state was a loose collection of organizations under the umbrella of the Iowa Farm Unity Coalition, which was formed in 1982. Its most activist elements—Catholic Rural Life and Prairiefire, whose executive director was an ordained minister—had some religious affiliation. The coalition also included farm organizations such as the American Agriculture Movement and the National Farmer's Union. All agreed on one central tenet, that agriculture must be reorganized to better meet the needs of farmers themselves rather than agribusiness.

In the firestorm that was the farm crisis before mobilization, however, there was an urgent need for the coalition to concentrate on nuts-and-bolts issues that nobody else was addressing. First, farm families in trouble needed to know their rights in the rapidly escalating confrontation with lenders. The coalition employed techniques developed over the sixties and seventies in urban activist organizations—hotlines with counselors, workshops, and demonstrations—to diffuse information about the implications of the downturn in the countryside.

One of the elements of the early success of the coalition was its understanding of the importance of media coverage of the plight of farmers. I witnessed one incident in the fall of 1985 that impressively illustrates this understanding and how it was implemented. During the debate over the new farm bill in the House of Representatives, one activist heard the news that her local congressman had voted against a key amendment designed to introduce mandatory controls for planting grain. Immediately she called a television station in Omaha and arranged for a crew to come out to her farm so that she could tape a statement. Within an hour a reporter and cameraman had driven the fifty-odd miles and set up their equipment. The interview was captured on videotape, and the crew drove away. The piece was the first item on the local news that evening.

Of course, media attention could be a two-edged sword. Television could beam its message great distances to influence viewers in the urban centers, but it is less clear how media attention played with the local population and with those whom advocates selected as specific targets of attention. The local neighborhood tended to be suspicious when one of their own rose against the norm and drew attention to herself or himself. Media attention could also prejudice official reaction where it mattered. On one occasion the state FmHA director attended a meeting with borrowers on the understanding that the media would not be present. He was frustrated to discover that both the television and print media were waiting for him when he made an appearance. The ease with which activists were able to utilize the media and the eagerness with which the media embraced the farm crisis had ramifications worth exploring.

The farm crisis obviously was an important story, full of human drama and emotion. But the reporting of events in progress inevitably generates some biases and inaccuracies that time and care might avoid. A case in point was the award of the Pulitzer Prize to a Des Moines *Register* photographer for his work on a photo essay published by the paper in December 1986. The *Register* was fairly tough on farm advocacy throughout the farm crisis. Although the paper gave very full coverage to events, editorially it was centrist, if not right of center on farm policy issues, and neopopulism often received short shrift. The photo essay, on the other hand, might well have been a neopopulist broadside, depicting as it did the travails of the dispossessed yeomanry.

The center of controversy was a picture, somewhat in the tradition of Dorothea Lange, of a jowly Small Business Administration official listening to the subject of the photo essay, a western Iowa farmer, at a hearing. Like Lange's famous shot of a potbellied white planter with his black field hands at a Mississippi country store, the Iowa picture suggested that evil forces were at work on an innocent victim.

The facts, however, were somewhat different as the official in the picture noted in a letter of protest:

> To inject some facts into the record. At the time the "picture" was taken, SBA had not laid a glove on these borrowers, to use a boxing term. It is a public record that these people were in a Chapter 11 bankruptcy from 1982 to 1984, which went nowhere and was eventually dismissed on that basis.

SBA made a disaster loan for $75,000 in January 1978 on which the annual payment of principal and interest for 1979 was made; the 1980 and 1981 payments were deferred by SBA, and up to 1982 some interest payments were made, with nothing after 1982.

SBA was only a passive defendant in the 1984-85 foreclosure that produced the home farm sale which was pictured in the essay and sealed their doom as family farmers. SBA had a first lien on a separate tract of land, but did not start foreclosure until 1987, which is still pending. The forebearance . . . spans some seven years.

Now how does that square with the inference of questionable "body language", charged insensitivity, and lack of agency compassion.[2]

Here a farm family, well known in western Iowa as being open about its problems—the husband had driven a tractor to Texas and back to draw attention to the farm crisis—had made itself available to a photojournalist for several months so he could record their foreclosure experiences as a permanent record of the times. Their willingness to participate in what amounted to a "theater of protest" was not typical farm family behavior. Although the actions of many lenders toward their clients were questionable, in this instance, as the letter pointed out, the SBA seems to have acted responsibly. It would seem, then, that the quest for publicity sometimes went a shade too far.

On the other hand, in the first years of the farm crisis, there was certainly a need to pursue stories of injustice vigorously. Before February 1985 the offices of Prairiefire in Des Moines acted as an intelligence center for gauging the severity of the downturn. Through the organization's hotline, counselors were not only able to dispense advice about strategies for dealing with debt problems but also to plot the seriousness of the situation on a county-by-county basis. Nothing was more dramatic than to listen to a distraught farmer or farm wife. The hotline, therefore, provided both intelligence and material for publicity that made Prairiefire an important force in the farm crisis. At least one prominent politician, Senator Charles Grassley, was moved by listening to a hotline conversation; partly as a result of this experience, he became an outspoken critic of the Farm Credit System and the Farmers' Home Administration.

It took many months, however, to override the conventional wisdom that farm problems were an isolated phenomenon af-

fecting only the poor managers.[3] Meanwhile, the telephone logs
at Prairiefire showed that a huge amount of psychological violence was being committed by nervous lenders on farm families.
Horror stories of sharp business practices designed to cover
losses were common. Farmers were tricked into signing documents that increased their obligations. Livestock and machinery
were seized without due process. In general farmers' rights were
trampled in the scramble to recover losses. The hotline recorded
it all, providing the coalition with credibility in the first years of
the crisis and helping to build contacts with the eastern press
and network television. In the long run the stories originating at
the hotline made their way to the large urban centers of the
country, where they helped influence public opinion.

As was the case in the sixties and seventies in urban America, a major part of the work of a grass-roots organization run by
professionals was the diffusion of beliefs and leadership roles to
the rank and file. The professionals hoped to establish a foundation on which the local people could build. The coalition began
with workshops and town meetings, but it soon became apparent that it was easier to train local counselors and clergy in crisis
intervention and financial and legal issues than to create grass-
roots initiative from scratch. In some communities where the
presence of important members was always felt, the coalition
had some success. But because the downturn was so selective,
only a certain segment of the farm population, those that were in
trouble, actively sought out the coalition. The most active leaders, thus, were usually farm men and women who had gone
through the wringer themselves, and membership, such as it
was, was not broadly based.

Therefore, although the coalition efficiently provided valuable free service to those in difficulties, in the short time available it was much less successful in its main goal of transforming
rural Iowa. Given the pervasive stigma attached to failure, the
only farmers who attended functions were the converted. The
Farmer-Rancher Congress in St. Louis in September 1986 was a
case in point. I attended two delegate-selection meetings in
different parts of Iowa; apart from the odd Farm Bureau partisan
sent by the parent organization as an observer, most of the dele-
gates had suffered financial setbacks of one kind or another.

The evidence from the farmers I interviewed shows that by the winter of 1986-87 most families untouched by the crisis were sympathetic to those who had suffered. On the other hand, this feeling did not translate into any desire to change the status quo. In contrast, activists who had some contact with the coalition or some similar organization were invariably militant about the injustices of the system and saw their own difficulties as a direct result of its failures.

In the long run the coalition's most lasting contribution came from their extensive knowledge of the problems farmers had with debt. From 1983 until the formulation of the Farm Credit System rescue plan in late 1987, coalition advocates were able to monitor and encourage developments for change in the farm-lending system. At first, lenders were hostile to forbearance in any form; in the end farm borrowers' aid was incorporated into the congressional legislation that authorized the Farm Credit System bailout.

The Establishment

Politics played a role in delaying state mobilization for the farm crisis. The presidential election of 1984 made it difficult for the Republican governor of Iowa to distance himself from the Reagan administration, postponing "profarmer" advocacy by politicians at the state level until 1985. That February a rally in Ames focused national attention on agriculture, and from then on the farm issue became sacrosanct. Every politican of whatever party gave farm issues careful attention.

For establishment organizations it was a case of positioning themselves to be of greatest benefit to their constituencies in the changed economic environment. Ironically the farm crisis created new opportunities for a variety of individuals and organizations. The Extension Service was a case in point. For the two previous decades utilization of the service had declined among farm families. Its all-out support of large-scale production agriculture designed for efficiency had suffered a heavy blow when so many "young tigers" who had followed this game plan fell from grace. Mobilization, therefore, provided an avenue for contact with a constituency that the Extension Service had previously missed or abandoned. The Farm Bureau, too, used the opportunities brought by the farm crisis wisely. Despite a loss of face over advocacy of big farming, its insurance programs, open to nonfarmers as well as farmers, kept membership high. In addition, the bureau bolstered its position among its farm membership through firm support of the farm program. In an uncertain world, standing up for the 1985 farm bill rather than for the more radical attempts to institute mandatory controls was a shrewd political strategy.

A test of the relative political influence of the Farm Bureau and the Iowa Farm Unity Coalition came in the primary election for secretary of agriculture in 1986. The candidate endorsed by the Iowa Farm Unity Coalition split the dissident vote in the Democratic primary with another antiestablishment rival, permitting another candidate, who had strong ties with state government, to win. In the general election, with the endorsement of the Farm Bureau, he trounced the Republican handily.

From the spring of 1985 the Cooperative Extension Service, through its toll-free long-distance hotline, became the initial contact agency for any Iowa farm family in difficulties. The aim of the service, funded initially by agribusiness, the Farmers' Home Administration, and the Farm Credit System, was referral rather than advocacy, as was the case with the Iowa Farm Unity Coalition. In essence counselors dispensed information farmers could use to plan their own strategy. They were told how to contact attorneys and other sources of help and information. Later, when funding came through state channels, these guidelines were extended. Staff lawyers were permitted to provide professional advice over the hotline, and counselors spent more time with clients discussing financial and legal problems.

Another area of contact with farmers at the grass-roots level came after the spring of 1986, when the mediation law passed the Iowa legislature. Lenders were then required to take cases before a member of the state-operated mediation service before they could foreclose on a farm family. The new law also stipulated that the farmer sit down with a staff associate of the Cooperative Extension Service and prepare his farm records for the mediation session. This was an opportunity for Extension to discuss crucial aspects of any farm operation with a hitherto neglected clientele. The staff associates were, by and large, farmers themselves, often graduates of Iowa State University who were recruited because of their educational qualifications. Their tool was a spread-sheet computer program designed to ask what-if questions about an operation. The program had little applicability to a farm operation in foreclosure or near bankruptcy. On the other hand, as an educational tool to encourage farmers to keep better records—a thrust of the Extension Service program for farmers in general—it had considerable scope.[4]

State-sponsored mediation was designed to bring the farm crisis to a resolution, to end much of the costly and fruitless litigation that had developed from 1983 to 1985. Although the program was not particularly successful in itself, it made a great contribution in encouraging negotiation between lenders and farmers. Threatened by official state mediation channels, borrowers and lenders were forced to work together.

By far the greatest number of cases in the best-organized mediation district in Iowa concerned the Farm Credit System. Out of these 159 were mediated between September 1986 and February 1987 with 58 percent ending in some kind of agreement. Of bank cases, 43 were mediated, of which 49 percent ended in agreement.[5] Unfortunately, early participants in the program complained of a total lack of commitment by the Farm Credit System, which treated mediation as an exercise in futility. Part of the reason for the failure of these cases was not only the intransigence of the lender but also lack of preparation by the borrower. Farmers often misunderstood mediation, believing that mediators were supposed to be advocates for farmers. The result was confusion and renewed bitterness among the farm families. Again the system seemed to be working against them.

The main objective of mediation was to cut through the confrontational stance on both sides. Farmers often came to sessions distraught about losing a farm that had been in the family for many generations and emotional about what the land meant to them. In contrast lenders were strictly business, unwilling to discuss anything but debt ratios and cash flow. Often they arrived "looking cool and rational," with the attitude that "it's your problem; if you don't come up with a plan that will work, we're going to liquidate."[6] In some instances negotiations involved more than two sides. Husbands and wives sometimes had different goals, and some creditors were willing to settle, while others were not.

The process can be illustrated by a simple case. In this instance the farmer's initial demand is for the lender to write off six thousand dollars of a fifty-thousand-dollar debt and reduce the interest rate on the note by 5 percent. If the bank refused, the farmer might threaten to take out a Chapter 11. The lender would blanch. He would make it clear that he was not used to having such demands made of him. It took a few hours for all sides to lower their voices and get beyond antagonism. Eventually they would make an agreement to reduce the debt and write-down the interest rate, though not by as much as the farmer first demanded.

Local Mobilization

At the local community level some kind of organization was also needed for those in stress from the downturn. The farm crisis struck individual communities with varying force and at different times. A community that suffered a bank failure was at greatest risk, for such a dramatic event affected both townspeople and farmers, depositors and borrowers. Less all-encompassing were individual bankruptcies and foreclosures, but if they came in any number, they too could begin to severely damage the economic stability of a community and force businesses to close.

Community farm crisis committees were ad hoc organizations in rural villages and towns united by the threat of economic failure. Having no permanent structure, they tended to wither away unless there was strong leadership and commitment. Ironically farmers were often less involved than townspeople, and typically when they did participate farmers had very specific goals. Many farmers complained that they disliked going to functions where all the news was bad. As long as they had no pressing problems themselves, they went their separate ways. In addition, with their busy schedules, most could not afford to attend too many meetings during the week.

Community activism usually worked best when it dealt with the emotional problems brought on by foreclosure or other catastrophes. Usually a pastor was behind this kind of mobilization, and much interdenominational liaison went on. Again, these committees were fairly short-lived or at least seasonal in their funcitoning. Finally, some locally sponsored financial and legal counseling also took place. This was usually conducted by private individuals—farmers who, through their own experience, had attained some knowledge of the law and farm finance.

But some communities did persevere with a farm crisis group of one sort or another for a considerable time. In Holstein, Ida County, the initial inspiration came from townspeople as much as farmers. In late 1984 the town held its first meeting, followed in January 1985 with speakers from a Nebraska community that had already had done some community organizing.[7] The Iowa Farm Unity Coalition sponsored a training session and public meeting in February 1985. Out of this came a farmer-dominated group that met every two weeks in the winter. This support group was remarkable for its longevity. It was still meeting in the early spring of 1987, and over the years had drawn participants from all over western Iowa and other states. The secret of its commitment was its core of members who had experienced unpleasant and protracted confrontations with lenders early in the farm crisis. In pursuit of their rights some had failed to find lawyers who were able to provide adequate answers to their particular problems, and as a result some had gone the pro se route of taking care of their own affairs in court. The common bond was confrontation with the establishment and the resolution of personal financial problems, rather than any desire to see improvement in the community.

The classic community trauma was bank failure. There were twenty three failures in the state from January 1985 until March 1987. In Sac County, where cattle losses and overexpansion in land caused much economic hardship, three banks failed in 1985. These failures were the result of the farm economy—a series of bad loans that became delinquent—rather than fraudulent management. All three banks opened the next day under new ownership—two became branches of larger banks—but the wreckage of failure took as much as twenty months to clear. Banks that failed before the summer of 1985 did not have the benefit of assistance from outside advocacy groups such as

Prairiefire or other neutral organizations. Depositors and borrowers had to face Federal Deposit Insurance Corporation officers who had little or no experience with agriculture and did not appreciate the seasonal nature of financial transactions for harvesting or planting. These banks were insured by the FDIC, and all depositors were eventually reimbursed up to the limit of a hundred thousand dollars. Borrowers, however, were not so fortunate, for the buyer of a closed bank had the option of picking up loans within thirty days. Those unclaimed then reverted to the portfolio of the FDIC for liquidation.

One of the three failed banks in Sac County closed its doors at Odebolt in April 1985.[8] Eighteen months later the implement dealer in town was no longer in business. In addition, the drug store, a hardware business, assorted clothing and shoe stores, and other businesses had closed. On main street the only establishments showing signs of life were the cafe, a television repair shop, the newspaper, a bar, an insurance agent, and a flower shop. Farmers who had tried to live with FDIC were giving up the fight and filing bankruptcy.

In the immediate aftermath of the closing, the community attempted to mobilize. The Methodist minister, together with colleagues in the ministerial association, attended meetings outside the community to learn what impact a bank failure could have on their congregations. From the Extension Service in the county seat, they got training intervention techniques and supplementary materials designed for this purpose.[9] In the summer of 1985 a meeting was held in the school for community members affected by the bank closing. That fall and winter there were other meetings for farm families in each congregation. Throughout this period ministers and priests stepped up their visiting schedules, accompanied each other on visits if necessary, and when one church was without a pastor for several months, shared the duties for this congregation.

The neighboring town of Early lost its bank in the fall of 1985. By then the state authorities and Prairiefire were better organized to counsel depositors about their rights.[10] Again those most vulnerable were farmers who had high-risk loans. For over a year several farmers tried to continue farming while doing monthly battle with the FDIC bureaucracy. The introduction of the Chapter 12 bankruptcy allowed some of them to cut their losses and seek other solutions. All in all, the community's contact with FDIC was unpleasant. The officers made no secret of their disgruntlement over being assigned temporary duty in some dusty prairie town. In Early they refused to eat their midday meal in the village, instead driving fourteen miles to a restaurant in a larger community to the north.

The specter of isolated farm families attempting to deal with overwhelming problems spurred the initiation of a statewide hotline. But however valuable, such a service was no substitute for personal visits by neighbors, relatives, and friends who would listen sympathetically during the difficult period after loss. Networks of peer listeners were available in several areas of the state. Their objective was to provide companionship during the most dangerous period after the loss of a farm. Once the family came to accept the loss, the danger of precipitous action had passed. Peer-group intervention, therefore, was a low-cost and efficient service. Usually those who had lost their farms, and with them their occupation, did not require elaborate therapy or other psychiatric assistance. What they needed was understanding and compassion while they lived through a period of readjustment and learned to go on to achieve more with their lives.

The Helping Professions

The mental health and spiritual needs of farmers were often neglected before the farm crisis. Their independence and their apparently strong family structure made them less likely to seek out professionals for help. Yet even before the crisis the farm family, and the intergenerational one in particular, hid an extraordinary amount of stress and tension behind a mask of "wellness." Once the crisis hit, the facade tended to crumble. Those families within reach of larger communities often had a mental health facility in easy reach and could count on professional assistance when it was needed. Farm families generally did not use social service agencies, however, and even after the crisis began in earnest, they maintained a certain resistance to outside intervention.

Social and mental health workers, therefore, had to approach farm families with a certain amount of caution. Early workshops, in which social workers tried to talk about emotional problems to middle-aged farmers, were not successful. The audience resented being talked down to and declared that outsiders were incapable of understanding the impact of the loss of a farm. Obviously, another approach was needed, and as with financial and legal counseling, the answer was found in peer involvement.

Here, the "circuit rider" system of delivering emotional assistance was one way to break down resistance. Farm women who had been through some of the same difficulties made regular visits to families who were going through tough times. Peer presenters and listeners possessed the necessary credibility to break down barriers and institute programs farm families could support. Their most difficult task was to grapple with the problem of change for those who left farming or had to greatly reduce their scale of operations, to persuade people to change their roles and values. Farm families had to learn that wives could take jobs off the farm, a family could be a family without working together, farms could be run without massive equipment, fathers need not feel guilty when they could no longer give the children chores to perform, and hard work would not solve every problem. Farmers had to overcome their own preconceptions and prejudices to resolve their difficulties.

The clergy in small communities had an equally difficult task in trying to reach farm families. Their job was complicated by the political climate of small towns. Pastors often had to be careful not to seem too activist oriented, for overemphasis on activism could alienate those members of their congregations who believed that farmers in financial difficulties had only themselves to blame. This fear was perhaps reflected by one survey early in the farm crisis in which 44 percent of respondents found their church "not at all supportive" of their needs and only 19 percent said their church "actively expressed support."[11] Obviously the farm crisis gave the clergy the opportunity to show that theirs was the authentic church. And despite the restrictions on their actions, thousands of clergy in rural Iowa parishes worked to make their responses to the rural crisis as utilitarian as possible.

One of the most powerful and best organized denominations was the Catholic church. Of course, many Protestant denominations—the Methodists and the Lutherans, for example—were equally forceful at the local level. The Catholic hierarchy, however, was alerted to the dangerous implications of change in the structure of American agriculture in the 1970s. The Catholic clergy, therefore, were able to be more outspoken than those of other denominations early in the crisis. The rural life directors of the four dioceses of Iowa were determined to help their congregations and the farm population in general to bring about positive results from the change they were quick to recognize. Their ministry was not designed for instant success but for the long haul.[12] One useful tool was the interdenominational retreat, which mixed spiritual uplift with nuts-and-bolts issues for those involved in farm failure. A large number of these were held throughout the state from 1983 onward.

As a result of the challenges brought on by the farm crisis, there was something of a renaissance in the rural church during these years. After decades of decline, its leaders and congregations saw that their institutions could contribute to the betterment of their communities, and the countryside benefited.

Lenders, Lawyers, and Farmers

The debt problem, both for individual farm families and for lenders, remained one of the principal themes of the farm crisis in Iowa. There was a triangular relationship among the farmer, the lender, and the attorney. These three interacted with one another from the time a problem loan was first identified through the final resolution, be it liquidation, bankruptcy, buy back, give back, renegotiation, or legal proceeding.

To understand the farm debt situation it is necessary to place it in the legal framework that attempted to deal with it, what has been termed the state remedies–bankruptcy system. The state courts form the first subsystem. Operating under state law, these courts oversee the mechanisms through which creditors seek payment—judgments, garnishments, attachments, or discovery. The other subsystem, bankruptcy, operates through the federal bankruptcy court primarily to protect debtors by preventing seizure of property by state courts, by extending the time for repayment of debts, and by discharging the debtor from liability for his debts.

The Bankruptcy Reform Act of 1978 attempted to modernize bankruptcy law and with it the subsystem, but despite some improvements, bankruptcy remained generally controversial, partly because the subsystem was never allowed to work as it was designed to do. In many cases the financial decay was already well advanced before a firm or an individual entered the halls of bankruptcy. "The bankruptcy court," it has been said, "deals not with businesses in financial difficulties, but with their skeletons, already picked clean by workouts, state court proceedings, informal liquidations, or merely the ravages of time and poor management."[13] Creditors preferred to work with the state subsystem, where they were better able to look after their own interests. For them bankruptcy was an expensive and unfamiliar process. Unlike the state system, which had courts in every county, the bankruptcy court was usually located in a distant city. In addition, a diligent creditor was capable of forcing a debtor to make "voluntary" payments in the state courts, whereas in bankruptcy assets were divided among competing creditors. As a result there was a strong perception among creditors that they were at a great disadvantage once a firm or individual reached the bankruptcy court. However, despite the lending industry's mistrust and the introduction of the new Chapter 12 farm bankruptcy provision in 1986, which lenders opposed, the fact remained that most firms and individuals who filed for reorganization under Chapter 11 or 12 did so under duress and were usually too late to affect the eventual outcome. In a real sense, then, the contest between debtor and creditor was always "zero sum" in bankruptcy.[14] In other words, no party came out a winner.

There was a certain irony in the way events unfolded in Iowa. In the initial stages of the crisis creditors had the upper hand in dealings with delinquent debtors. Desperate to defray losses, however, they pursued debtors assiduously in the state courts, forcing farm families to seek the only protection available: bankruptcy.

Farmers were always vulnerable to pressure from outsiders.

The structure of modern agriculture, which required a large number of inputs, gave salesmen scope for the exercise of their powers of persuasion. Farmers were at an even greater disadvantage when dealing with professionals, who, with much education and more polish than the average farmer, seemed so superior. While the economy was roaring along, farmers often allowed their bankers to dictate operational strategies to them. In view of the large sums of money involved, it is perhaps not surprising that lenders wanted to restrict how the funds were used, but their relationship with borrowers was never the symbiotic partnership that banks liked to advertise. Once danger signs in the economy appeared, the banker-farmer business relationship was revealed in its true colors—and confrontation rapidly developed. A farmer's response could take one of several courses, but whatever the choice, some kind of legal assistance was sought.

Bank control theory presumes that banks, with their "ability to grant and refuse loans, to extend leverage . . . and dictate policies to customers," are central to the power structure of business.[15] The farm crisis provides an unusual opportunity to study this institutional power and its effects on farm clients. I have already shown that in many cases banks overreacted in their efforts to regain huge losses from farm customers. In their keenness to redeem themselves, however, lenders succeeded in destroying their business relationships with many farmers. At the same time, countervailing forces affected the noncommercial sector of farm finance, notably the Farmers' Home Administration. A series of judicial decisions beginning in 1983 permitted borrowers to remain in farming even though their loans were nonperforming. Although Production Credit of the Farm Credit System also acted swiftly to redeem losses from 1983 onwards, the Land Bank was frustrated in its desire to do the same by political action—in Iowa with the institution of moratoria—and class action litigation.

Because rural banking remained relatively competitive before and during the farm crisis, the control over customers by loan officers was nowhere near as rigid as theory would suggest. Before the downturn, farmers left one institution for another to obtain longer lines of credit. During the crisis they left the Land

Bank to receive lower interest rates for long-term loans at local banks. This was a new development, for local banks had not encouraged the support of long-term mortgages since before World War I. Finally, farmers increasingly turned to cash and self-financing for their needs—for those who were able to do it, the ultimate answer to lending institutions who had abused their power over farm clients.

Of the eighteen banks in the four counties of the study area, only about half would be classified as farm banks (making over 50 percent of their loans to agriculture), but all depended on the health of the agricultural economy to prosper. All but one were making money in 1983. Two years later most had lower incomes or were actually losing money. Four banks failed in 1985, although they had their bad years in 1984. Probably the best indicator of an institution's health was the ratio of its troubled debt to its capital—in theory the lower the ratio the better the health of the bank. Some conservative banks had very low debt ratios because they rarely loaned money to local people but preferred to invest in bonds and securities. Others purposely loaned out a large proportion of their deposits to farmers and business people because they felt an obligation to assist the community. Until 1985 the debt ratios continued to grow, but they had declined by 1986 because bank officers pruned and wrote off much of their farm debt in any way they could, with the bank examiners forcing the liquidation of nonperforming accounts. Farm families often suffered in this process. For most of the banks this medicine seemed to work; only five continued to lose money in 1986. One of these had a worse year in 1986 than in 1984, and had continually lost money throughout the middle eighties. Fortunately that bank belonged to the owner of the Minnesota Twins, who could afford to absorb the red ink.[16]

During the mobilization process bankers learned many lessons about how to treat their customers. According to an article published in the *United States Banker*, prudent institutions used committees to decide when to terminate a loan; it would be "foolish to think that any loan officer had the emotional control necessary" to perform this unpleasant task alone. Files were kept clean of negative memos, in case they were subpoenaed. Loans were never terminated suddenly. Officers tried to make good faith a course of conduct and did their best to obtain as much information as possible about a farm business. Whether these pronouncements were correct for Iowa is impossible to tell. However, even in the smallest rural banks presumably, some harsh lessons of the past were absorbed.[17]

Certainly before mobilization lenders made little effort to negotiate with farm borrowers. The hard-nosed approach, intended to recoup losses, made it very difficult for farmers who still had some assets and wanted to remain in farming. Without much room for maneuver, farmers could only file a Chapter 11 to ward off an institution bent on obtaining assets. Unfortunately, Chapter 11 was an expensive procedure not designed for a farm operation caught in the downturn, and it had little chance of success.[18]

The only other option, full bankruptcy, Chapter 7, left creditors with a file of uncollectable debts. There could be little possibility of continuing to farm and eventually repaying creditors. In a small community, where unsecured short-term debt was the common way of doing business, most farmers believed very deeply in trying to avoid the ignominy of default. They knew that failure to pay could put their neighbor out of business. Therefore, most avoided Chapter 7 if at all possible.

It was easier to be confrontational when lenders were not local. This was possibly one of the reasons that the Farm Credit System had so much difficulty with farmers. But regardless of the type of institution, the job of being an agricultural loan officer was singularly unpleasant, and there was a high turnover rate.

For farmers in financial difficulty filing for bankruptcy or the serving of a foreclosure notice initiated a long period of waiting. This state of limbo was created by regulations that permitted a farm family one year to find resources to buy back their property after a foreclosure. Bankruptcies also moved glacially toward resolution. The slowness of litigation, of course, did have some advantages. In the tempo of the farm crisis, the longer a family could delay, the better the prospects of achieving a settlement to their satisfaction.

The triangular relationship among attorney, lender, and farmer came together most dramatically in court, particularly

over bankruptcy negotiations. One case selected at random aptly
illustrates the many issues involved in a typical Chapter 11
bankruptcy.[19] This case involved a middle-aged dairy farmer
from northeast Iowa, one of those who was demographically and
occupationally at greatest risk. He had filed in 1985 through his
attorney in the county seat. His creditors, which included the
Land Bank, the local Production Credit Association, and John
Deere, had all rejected his reorganization plan, but because of the
sheer weight of other cases in the court, he continued farming
until the summer of 1986 while his attorney filed monthly
financial statements with the judge.

In September 1986 he was summoned to another hearing.
His creditors intended to push ahead with their liquidation
proceedings and to disperse whatever equity remained to their
institutions. For his part, the dairyman had seen his life fall apart
since filing. His wife had left him and he was in poor physical
and psychological health. His doctor had recently diagnosed
diabetes, discovered quite by chance when a lawyer from Minneapolis with experience in medical law was asked by the farmer's attorney for an opinion. She noticed that he had a tendency
to nod off to sleep during the interview, a probable sign of
diabetes.

In any event, at the hearing in bankruptcy court in September 1986 the dairyman was represented by the Minneapolis
lawyer. The attorneys representing the creditors expected a
short, routine hearing. They were surprised when the dairymen's
counsel made her opening statement. Her client, she said, was
incompetent to look after his own affairs. He was both mentally
and physically unable to make the decisions required of a businessman in bankruptcy. Thus, like a minor in probate, he needed
a guardian to administer his bankruptcy.

The other attorneys were taken aback. They raised their eyes
to the ceiling as if to say they had now heard everything there
was to hear in a farm bankruptcy court. The judge also seemed
surprised and called a recess in order to consult case law. Outside in the corridor the creditors' attorneys tore into the farmer's
counsel. One was particularly disgusted. He was there, he said,
to collect a paltry fifteen hundred dollars worth of machinery for
John Deere, and she was wasting his and the court's time with

frivolous motions that made the northern district of Iowa bankruptcy court look like a welfare agency.

When the judge returned, he asked the attorney to continue her presentation. She suggested that because of her client's condition it would be beneficial for him to continue milking his cows. This she said was the best therapy for a man whose personal and occupational life lay shattered. Again, the eyes of the lawyers shot up to the ceiling. They consulted among themselves hurriedly, and then the PCA lawyer rose to make a statement for them all. He pointed out that the case had remained unsettled for fifteen months. They could appreciate his problems, but the dairyman had shown himself incapable of abiding by the terms of his own plan of reorganization. Their clients had waited so long for reimbursement that assets would pay back not even thirty cents on the dollar. He therefore asked the judge to dismiss the petitioner's arguments, which were but attempts to delay the case further.

The judge then made his presence felt for the first time. He agreed with the attorney that the case needed to be resolved, but he also believed that the dairyman had some legitimate rights that ought to be carefully weighed. The question of guardianship could not be decided immediately because of the legal precedent it would establish. He therefore postponed ruling on that matter for a month. On the other hand, it was time to decide whether or not the farmer could continue. While it is a comparatively simple matter to vacate foreclosed property and move machinery, removing livestock and caring for them in the interim is more difficult.

Eventually the lawyers finished their haggling and a compromise was reached. The dairyman would move to his mother's home in town. At the same time he would surrender the farm's keys to the Land Bank, the machinery to John Deere, and the cows to PCA. The latter would arrange for a trucker to pick up the livestock and transport them to the sale barn in the county seat. They would be lodged there, fed and milked by a sale barn employee, until the next auction date.

These, briefly, were some of the human, financial, legal, and logistical problems that confronted lenders, attorneys, and farm families on thousands of different occasions during the farm crisis. It is easy to understand the frustration lenders felt when their plans were stymied by legal maneuvering, and just as easy to understand the sorrow of fifty-year-old farmers who saw their only possible livelihood slipping away, seized by a collusion of powerful forces. More often than not, the only winners in such a scenario were the lawyers.

Country lawyers attempted to catch up with the intricacies of agricultural law, especially its debtor code, but the complex interrelationships of the courthouse square made conflict of interest a possibility in cases involving local farmers, local banks, and local lawyers. Therefore, many cases were eventually referred to attorneys in other communities for action.[20] The evidence suggests that the void in the practice of agricultural law was filled by those who worked in other areas. The climate of confrontation encouraged those with trial and bankruptcy experience to move into the agricultural field, fueling the litigious atmosphere between farmers and lenders.

Despite the efforts of the Iowa Bar Association, which formed its own agricultural law committee in late 1984 to advise its members and farmers, occasionally situations developed that the organization could not control. Some attorneys were unprofessional. There were the inevitable complaints of fee gouging, especially when a Chapter 11 case reverted to a Chapter 7. Large up-front fees did not always bring the kind of service they merited. Senior partners in law firms became overextended and pushed work off onto less-qualified junior colleagues. At least one attorney was so overwhelmed by his huge case load that he simply packed up and left Iowa. Another, who had a number of clients in the sample, preferred to get paid in kind rather than in cash. On the surface this looked to be a satisfactory arrangement for those with limited liquid assets, but in practice it created a number of misunderstandings and much bitterness.[21]

Eventually the passage of time, the expense of litigation, and the frustrations of dealing with an agricultural economy that refused to improve made it obvious to all parties involved that negotiation was preferable to confrontation. Mandatory mediation was a step in this direction. Unfortunately, by the time this realization came, far too many Iowa farm families had wasted precious resources trying to save themselves through methods that, partly for institutional, partly for economic, and partly for human reasons, were doomed to failure. Eventually a resolution to the debt problem was worked out—at least on paper.

Perhaps nothing epitomized the transformation of the debt problem better than the bailout of the Farm Credit System. Signed into law by President Reagan in the first week of January 1988, this action vividly expressed how far the process of mobilization to deal with the downturn had traveled in Iowa and the nation since the early days of 1983. Nationally, the system received $4 billion in aid, but at a stiff price. The bankrupt Omaha district, of which Iowa was part, was forced to merge with St. Paul, thus saving millions in administrative costs. From the viewpoint of the indebted farm family the most important provisions in the legislation were the institutionalization of aid for borrowers. Many of the issues for which the Iowa Farm Unity Coalition had lobbied over the years—a fair review process, the right of a previous owner to purchase or rent land that was lost to the system, the disclosure of interest rates, and the establishment of mediation, for instance—were officially sanctioned.[22]

5

Survival

Although the downturn was selective, it did not differentiate between the well-to-do and the less well established farm family. All took part in the general expansion of the seventies to some extent, but the timing of their actions was most important. Some bought land before the steepest inflation, or their children were too young to begin farming in the boom. These the crisis spared while it savaged others. Among those who did have problems, family solidarity, off-farm jobs, the farm program, and the wise use of still-available resources all gave a family some hope of putting their lives together again.

Farm families were used to blending their lives to the rhythms of nature. Even their debts were tied to the passage of the seasons. After harvest they paid back the lenders; before planting they sought to refinance. The slow pace with which their fate unfolded was maddeningly frustrating, but it was part and parcel of an occupation in which crucial decisions were made far in advance. Families found themselves twisting in the wind between November and the following April, waiting for a decision on financing for the next crop year. Even more stressful was the extreme length of time it took to resolve the financial problems of those in trouble. By the early months of 1987, fifty-three of the sample families had gone through reorganization and were still farming in some fashion, their financial problems as yet unresolved. Yet nearly half of these reorganizations had taken place more than two years before, and some had been waiting since 1983 (Table 14). Only in the fall of 1986 was there much movement for these families to resolve these difficulties. One of the aims of this chapter is to explore how this limbo existence came into being and how families who were active and busy around the farm only a year or so before were able to tolerate such a condition. One young farmer, whose father's estate owed

Table 14. Unresolved Reorganizations, Spring, 1987

Period Since Reorganization	Percentage of Reorganizations	Number of Reorganizations
Under six Months	6	2
Six months to one year	11	6
One to two years	41	22
More than two years	43	23

Source: Sample data.

the Farmers' Home Administration almost a million dollars, summed up the situation succinctly. "A guy," he said, "gets immune after a while."

Family Solidarity

Not surprisingly, members of the extended family, such as grandparents and uncles, played an important role in survival. Farm families had always utilized familial resources, and the farm crisis proved this kind of behavior to be as vital as it was earlier in the century. For generations, families had borrowed and lent money among themselves, and the downturn intensified these practices.[1] Indeed, it was encouraged by lenders in their drive to squeeze liquid assets out of borrowers. Elderly widows were encouraged to cash in their certificates of deposit and apply the proceeds to solving their children's debt problems.

Research on farm families—some of it done before the downturn—emphasized conflict within the family during times of great stress.[2] While certain families did suffer from intra-and intergenerational and marital conflict (their problems will be discussed later), by and large those in trouble were remarkably free of familial problems (Table 15). Without continuous participant observation it would be impossible to judge the strains on a marriage or the frustrations that might flare up between a father and son in the course of living and working together. Certainly, however, during the interviews the families appeared supportive of each other. Whatever differences they had seem to have been forgotten under the stress of lender pressure. In addition all the

Table 15. Familial Conflict during the Farm Crisis

	Percentage Experiencing	Number Experiencing
No family conflict	65	88
Intragenerational conflict	14	19
Intergenerational conflict	14	19
Divorce	7	7

Source: Sample data.

divorces were in the younger generation, and only half were attributed directly to the farm crisis.

In two-generation farm families the most likely form of intergenerational conflict resulted from a failure of the younger generation that put the senior generation in jeopardy. Such conflict was intensified by attitudinal differences between father and son. Typically, the parents, growing up in the Depression, had been taught extreme frugality, only to see their operation being sacrificed by what they considered the profligacy of their children. In the sample families, however, this pattern was uncommon.

Intragenerational conflict most often originated from the division of an estate. At the same time, long years of experience had made many wary of sibling partnerships, especially when the children of brothers who operated together, were becoming old enough to farm. A number of families had solved this dilemma before the downturn and so avoided the conflict.

Even where conflict existed there were strong practical reasons for forging a united front against outside pressures. Each generation had an interest in the farm and especially the land. Just before the elections in the fall of 1986, when the Land Bank at last showed signs of willingness to negotiate, the governor selected a northwest Iowa family in the sample to test some of the legal precedents that were blocking settlement in thousands of cases. This family was chosen partly because of political connections but, more important, for its demographic and financial profile. It was a father-son partnership on a century-old farm, homestead in the 1870s. The parents had retired to town, leaving the son and his schoolteacher wife on the home place. The purchase of some high-priced but not very productive land in the late seventies, poor cattle prices, and crop losses made it impossible for them to keep up with the land payments. By 1985 the Land Bank had foreclosed and seemed bent on taking over the homestead as well. During the period of the foreclosure, and especially after the governor's lawsuit and the negotiations that followed, the family members were extraordinarily supportive of one another. Off-farm heirs came long distances to visit, and closer to home, the farmer son drove into town every day to eat lunch with his parents. For their part, there was never any question that they would take care of the large deficiency payment once a settlement was worked out with the Land Bank. This bonding in times of adversity was celebrated in the following spring after the negotiations produced a resolution of all the stress and tension. Then all the men of the family hosted a picnic for the women before departing for the wilds of Canada on a fishing trip.

The closing of ranks was expressed in other ways as well. If land could not be kept in the immediate family, sometimes close relatives were able to take over ownership. This scenario transpired in the case of an east-central Iowa cattle feeder who was forced to give land back to a Minneapolis finance company. During the negotiations, the finance company agreed to sell the land to the farmer's uncle, a lawyer in Florida. In another instance the purchaser of foreclosed land was a father-in-law, a school administrator at the other end of the state. In other cases a brother-in-law and a daughter saved land from being returned to the lender by putting up the necessary cash for siblings and parents.

Some of this assistance was surreptitious, designed to prevent a possible deterioration of relationship within the family. One sample father had three children in some form of difficulty; he was forced to perform an intricate juggling act to transfer funds to a daughter and son-in-law in order to pay off the PCA without the knowledge of his two sons, who had also received assistance of one kind or another. Reaching out to a son-in-law in self-inflicted financial difficulty was something of an acid test for family solidarity. In one family when this happened, the other children joked that their sister had gotten her inheritance a little early.

At the same time, assistance to children in difficulties was an obvious sacrifice for parents. One man who failed early borrowed money from his parents in 1983 because he wanted to remain in farming. Three years later he probably regretted this decision. Nevertheless, both husband and wife were determined to pay back everything owed to their elderly parents. Both took off-farm jobs, as well as working the farm when they could find the time.

Most parents remained understanding and reasonably fair-minded. One father, having bailed out two of his sons, declared, "We would help the boys again if the need arose." In only one case did an elderly parent refuse to make any allowances for his son's mistakes after his expansion had caused him to lose virtually everything. His refusal to intervene brought about the dominolike collapse of a family operation that also included the grandchildren. Much more typical were the parents who believed that if they had the resources, they should try to help their children—even their middle-aged children. One poignant case concerned a farm that had roots going back five generations. The son had succumbed to expansion fever. The old father recounted that his wife was disconcerted when she discovered that he intended to put up $125,000 to satisfy some of his son's creditors, but the father was not particularly bothered by this potential loss. What would be devastating, he said, was the loss of the hundred-year-old farm. Only a hint of bitterness toward his son was detectable: "Bob," he conceded, "had learned a lot." This generation was able to maintain its equanimity while losing substantial assets to children because it had seen economic disaster before. The elders knew that farming was a gamble in the best of times, and landed wealth transient. The remark of yet another father about the loss of 160 acres to an insurance company after his son got into difficulties captured this attitude. "I started with nothing," he exclaimed, "and I'll probably end with nothing."

But to dwell solely in the financial aspects of family interaction, however important, would be to misrepresent the total picture. In 28 percent of the sample families two generations shared the same acreage or lived within walking distance of each other. Some parents lived in town and traveled out to the farm every day. Thus, there was very close and continuous contact between parents and children. Years of dealing with each other by keeping emotions under control were good preparation for times of extreme stress. In one family the parents drove over to breakfast every morning to their children's almost new home, which both generations knew was the cause of their financial difficulties. Another elderly father came out to the farm every day, even though his son-in-law had suffered a major loss. He insisted on showing a visitor around the well-appointed home with its spectacular bathrooms not, as might be supposed, to demonstrate his son-in-law's lack of judgment but rather as a gesture of pride in his children.

Families not only provided material and psychological support. In one case they gave a good deal more. Several family members formed their own country band. Performance fees injected some badly needed financial remuneration when it was needed most. More important, the band was an emotional and artistic outlet for the members. On Saturday nights when the band played in local taverns, the family could create something together and give others pleasure at the same time. Without the band their lives would have been bleak indeed.

Case Studies in Survival

On the surface, rural Iowa seems a most egalitarian society, and boom and bust further blurred differentiation. Nevertheless, such subtle distinctions as did endure were useful in analyzing farmers' response to their unfortunate predicament. Upper-class families were particularly vulnerable because of their previous high status. There was a kind of universal glee in the community when "the big shots" fell on their faces. Still, prominent farmers who got into trouble had more resources to fall back on than did their less fortunate peers. Most had a network of relatives and friends far from the immediate neighborhood. So it was possible to remove themselves on occasion to relieve tension. But like everyone else in a similar position, the well-to-do had a strong need to keep up the pretense of normal existence as best they could. Perhaps there is one generalization applicable to upper class farmers: the stigma of failure seemed to remain with them longer than with others under the same pressure.

In November 1986 I interviewed one such family. According to local gossip and archival research, the family had lost a large amount of land in the recent past. I half expected to be turned down, but as it turned out the farmer agreed to sit down and talk. He seemed relieved to be able to discuss his past with a stranger. At the time of the interview he had been struggling to come to grips with his changed circumstances for three years. One of his chief concerns was to shield his children from the true nature of the family's position—in other words, to keep up appearances until better times returned. This need was brought home a few days later when I was invited to lunch. We sat down to the kind of meal that would have received a very favorable review from the restaurant critic at a large metropolitan daily. Both husband and wife seemed to enjoy the visit. One could only assume that they were pulling out all the stops to impress and also to reassure each other yet again that they could carry on as if nothing had happened.

Both were graduates of exclusive eastern schools; they had met at one of the weekend mixers that were customary before Ivy League schools became coeducational. By chance, both their families had originated in the same western Iowa town. While one patriarch stayed in the locality to farm, the other had gone to college and then migrated to California to become a state forester. After marriage they returned to the small town where the husband's father was farming and set about carving an empire out of the prairie. They began with a sizable number of tracts from the older generation, and expanded to almost five thousand acres by 1979. The husband's father lived with his son's family in their modern compound complete with tennis court, but the younger generation had total autonomy. In the seventies, farming was stimulating and profitable. The grain, hog, and cattle operation seemed a model of its kind, and with several employees to look after the livestock, the family could afford an active social life. At certain slack times in the year they could slip off to the West Coast, visit relatives, and take a break from farming.

This ideal existence was shattered in 1983 by a series of

financial and familial setbacks. First, an elevator bungled a grain storage contract. This snafu in turn caused problems with the Commodity Credit Corporation. Loss in land equity and difficulties with land payments made 1984 a difficult year. As was common at this stage of the farm crisis the family became a target of their creditors' desire to recoup losses. But unlike others, who fought aggressive lenders with Chapter 11 bankruptcy, they attempted to negotiate with the bankers, the Land Bank, and the insurance companies that held the mortgages on the land. One bank, in trouble itself, stopped their checks and so began a chain reaction that prevented the payment of rent and delayed the soybean harvest.

By the fall of 1984 the supports of this empire were beginning to buckle under the dead weight of debt. Between 1977 and 1982 the farmer had borrowed over $7 million. The family began negotiations with the Prudential Insurance Company to take back large blocks of land. It was an attempt to proceed in orderly fashion, but the Land Bank, John Deere, and two local banks refused to wait their turn and also began to serve judgments on the family.

As if outside pressure were not enough, the farm couple also had to endure internal family dissension. An elder sister had come back to live in the community in the seventies. A career woman who had some experience in business, she looked askance at the situation in 1983-1984. It seemed to her that the family would lose everything to its creditors, and because she also held an interest in the business, she determined to halt the slide. Leaving the family lawyer, she engaged a new attorney who advised her to take out Chapter 11 bankruptcy. In addition, she insisted as part of the family's reorganization plan that her brother hand over his home to her, and move to another. The move occured during the worst harassment from lenders. Ironically, the strategy proved to be ill founded, and by the end of 1986, the brother, who had opted for negotiation, looked to be in a somewhat more favorable position than his sister. In any event, the debacle and resulting disagreements over the rescue of the business caused a total break in relations between siblings.

From 1985 the farm operation was in limbo. Without credit to put in a crop, the couple had to skimp and scrounge to find resources. Now, there were only a few head of custom-fed cattle in the huge lots that had once been full of their own animals. Five hundred acres, held in a family trust and thus protected from the clutches of the lenders, were all that remained of the thousands once owned.

The failure of a business is an unnerving experience for anyone, but the failure of a farm, part of which was inherited, was even more ignominious. Even more humiliating was that the farmer's father lived to see this loss. How did the family survive this ordeal? In this family it was the wife who was able to grow in stature and to discover a new role for herself. For years she had been satisfied with her duties as homemaker and nurturer. Now she became the dominant member of the household and active in community affairs. Without her leadership and support, her husband might have suffered a complete breakdown. The farm crisis that ruined her husband's career gave his wife a new dimension and meaning.

One of the characteristics of the farm crisis was the failure of farmers in the early stages to form a united front against the onslaught of lenders. Perhaps this was not altogether surprising in view of the intensely personal nature of financial difficulty in any form and the intensely individual nature of farming. More-over, one's loss was usually another's gain. Yet there were farmers with influential positions in the state agricultural establishment who were well aware of the danger signals in the early eighties. In 1983, for example, a prominent east-central Iowa farmer found colleagues on the state Farm Bureau board would not listen to his warnings about the possible effect of the downturn of the farm economy. At that time his own operation was already suffering, and a serious hog disease caused a further setback. His response was to place some land on the market, but unfortunately there was no buyer.

A brave front to the outside world helped him and his wife hide their growing anxiety. The wife was an expert on farm office management, who had published a book on the subject. In the very year they began to think seriously of liquidating their farm, she appeared on the front cover of a national farm magazine. In the end a close friend's suicide over farm-related losses gal-vanized them into action to try to save what was left of the business. Realizing that their principal lenders were unlikely to approve a hastily drawn reorganization plan, they employed all their professional skills to put together a workable arrangement that had some hope of success with the most intransigent lender.

They used their own computers to generate cash flow charts that would help them decide what to sell. The vacation home in Missouri was obviously first to go. Other sales were not so simple. It was both difficult and extremely stressful to try to sell farmland while its value was plummeting. The deed holder, the Land Bank, was far from eager to negotiate, and the situation was complicated by liability for deferred estate taxes on the land. Even with modern tools it was not easy to work through this morass. Eventually, however, after almost a year of bargaining, the Land Bank came to terms in August 1986, agreeing to take some land back and accepting a deficiency judgment of a hundred thousand dollars.

Thus one of the more professional farm families in the state spent three years under pressure. Only by using resources and talent that few others possessed were they able to persevere to resolution. It is little wonder that thousands of others were less fortunate.

Most farmers had always responded to financial difficulties by working harder, but in the 1980s the traditional substitution of labor for capital would not work. Crippling losses in the cattle business plagued one large operator in the late seventies and early eighties. A one-hundred-year record of farming in the community was evidence that cattle had been good to the family in the past. By the seventies, however, when the son took over from his father, the old ways of operating, and especially marketing, were outdated. Competition from western feedlots left Iowa cattle feeders at a disadvantage. Intergenerational conflict exacerbated a risky environment. In 1983 accumulated cattle losses and drought brought a bad situation to a head. Finally, the farmer reached the realization that he had failed. Standing in a cornfield in August 1983, surrounded by wilting cornstalks, he saw that there would be no harvest that year, and he had not participated in the payment-in-kind program. It was a fatal blow. Since 1977 the cattle enterprise had ridden a roller coaster. Losses had forced refinancing, but by 1983 this debt cost seventeen dollars an hour to service. That year, while the farm grossed $1.6 million, it suffered a net loss of $450,000. In the fall of 1983 the farmer gave back twenty-five hundred acres in an effort to satisfy creditors. All that remained were some parcels in trust to the cattle feeder's mother.

For him there was never any question that he would remain in farming in some capacity. To this end he signed a contract to custom feed cattle in his lots for a group of local investors. In essence, as he was fully aware, he became a hired manager on his own farm. He used his own machinery and facilities to work for a group of off-farm investors who could use this service as a tax write-off. The farmer blamed himself for his troubles. He recognized that he had opted for one of the more exploitative business arrangements in farming because he could not face leaving for something else. If nothing else, the hard work and long hours made him forget his predicament, and cattle were, in any case, the only life he knew.

The main casualty was his wife. Hindsight suggested that this family had missed an opportunity to leave farming several years before, and this city girl would gladly have quit. As it was, she spent her days in the farm office weighing cattle trucks full of livestock and trying to keep abreast of the voluminous paper work required to keep track of hundreds of cattle belonging to others. Their changed situation found her doing more, not less, than before on the farm—this at a time when she needed to distance herself from the cause of so much distress over the previous decade. While she loyally supported her husband's goal of getting back into farming for himself, she remained ambivalent about their situation. One had to wonder how long she could keep up this stoicism. Like most farmers, this family frowned on psychological help and considered it bad form to discuss business and family problems with outsiders. Functioning for so long without a domestic split or more serious consequences demonstrated considerable tenacity.

Overall, among the sample families who got into trouble, nearly as many made some initial effort at negotiation with the lender as took a fighting stance (48 percent to 52 percent). As the farm crisis gathered momentum, the diffusion of information about farmers' rights improved the chances of protecting property. Nevertheless, in the long haul it was unclear whether fighting a lender was any more productive than cooperating. Some fought because they had no alternative; others used this strategy to move the bank into a negotiating stance; still others were victims of their attorney's lack of judgment.

For example, one very energetic farmer who had become one of the largest operators in his community entirely by his own efforts, brought four sons and a son-in-law into farming in the seventies. Fortunately, he was prudent enough to make them all independent operators. So that when one of the sons could not make the payments on a parcel of his land, the father was able to maneuver and shield himself and the other members of the family. The standard practice of the Land Bank in this situation was to try to recoup some of its losses by moving aggressively against a large family operation. By issuing foreclosure notices and refusing to negotiate, the Land Bank hoped not only to obtain the land for its portfolio but also to capture the full deficiency payment due on the transaction.[3] In this instance, the son and his father tried to persuade the Land Bank to take the parcel back. Negotiations proved fruitless, however, and when officers threatened foreclosure and seemed bent on moving against other pieces of family property, the son declared bankruptcy; and the father hired a lawyer with a solid reputation for winning debtor cases. Eventually, when the climate for negotiations changed and it was no longer in the interest of the Land Bank to pursue the case, a settlement was worked out.

Other families were caught up in the spiral of ever-increasing interest rates. One of the Land Bank's reactions to losses was to force up interest rates on most borrowers, especially those with the least likelihood of being able to tolerate the increases. The only way many borrowers could hope to continue servicing their debt was to be excused the payments on principal for the duration of the crisis and to have interest rates lowered. When the Land Bank introduced a policy of variable rates dependent on the financial condition of the customer, some families left the institution, but those in poor financial condition did not have this option. One sample family tried to withhold payments in the winter of 1986, in the hope of forcing negotiations and a reassessment of their position. Unfortunately, the family calculated wrong, and the Land Bank began foreclosure proceedings.

A number of families were affected by a bank closing in their community and spent the next fifteen months trying to deal with the rigid rules of the Federal Deposit Insurance Corporation. Even one farmer who did not have a loan with the failed bank was caught up, for he had sold machinery and other property to someone else who did. After over a year of haggling while his own financial position deteriorated, he decided that the quickest method of solving these problems was to leave farming and liquidate his operation through a Chapter 7 bankruptcy. A neighbor who was a borrower at the failed institution had to endure the intransigence of the FDIC for over a year because he wanted to stay on the farm. He managed to hold out until the initiation of the new Chapter 12 bankruptcy provision and filed in January 1987.

Some families had the bad luck to fail at the wrong time, while the attorneys were recommending Chapter 11 bankruptcy. Those who took this bad advice made a costly error. One dairyman, for example, was almost fifty and apprehensive about getting an off-farm job. Because he wanted to continue farming, he filed for Chapter 11. Nine months later, after the expenditure of over twenty thousand dollars, he took full bankruptcy and began working as a laborer for a neighbor.

Ironically, a sudden death or a tragic accident could sometimes dramatically reverse the fortunes of an intergenerational farm family in trouble. One father suffered a heart attack while spreading manure on a springlike winter day. He fell from his tractor, and his body was crushed when the machine ran over him. Over-expansion in the seventies and farm losses by one of the sons had placed considerable pressure on this enterprise. However, at one stroke the death resolved these problems through the payment of ample life insurance benefits.

At least one sudden loss in a family may have been due to the stress of trying to save the farm. This death from a heart attack demonstrated that the Iowa farm crisis was not especially kind even to those who had impeccable establishment credentials. The family head had not only been the farm aide to a Republican congressman, he was also on the state conservation board and was well known and respected in his county and the state as a whole. One of his sons had married an Extension Service home economist. Like many others, the family had expanded to bring two sons into farming in the seventies. The family had bought land and borrowed money to modernize livestock facilities. It would be correct to say that the father was totally unprepared for the kind of pressure the Farm Credit System exerted when it became clear that he and his sons could not continue making the scheduled payments. Here was a farmer who was community oriented all his career—he had served on both the PCA and Land Bank boards in the past—but despite the attention he had paid to civic responsibilities, he was getting no more consideration than the next man. While attending a state conservation meeting in Des Moines just before Christmas 1986, he collapsed and died shortly afterward in the hospital. His sons and widow could not be blamed for believing that the unyielding behavior of the Farm Credit System was partly responsible for their loss. Neither could they take much comfort from the fact that the business would stay afloat because of it.

Undoubtedly the successful resolution to any kind of reorganization required an iron will, great stamina, and considerable financial acumen and resources. One east-central Iowa cattle feeder was able to survive partly because of the careful planning he did before he even took out a Chapter 11. Actions taken long before, in the seventies, in some measure ensured that he and his family, unlike some who went this route, had some chance of pulling through. Partly because of fears that inheritance taxes would gobble up his property, he had transferred his home to his wife and some of his land to a son. These "hidden assets" were shielded from the grasp of marauding lenders when the downturn came. This farmer prided himself on his business oriented approach to agriculture and knew he would need the best representation possible in the coming battle with lenders. He employed not only a Chicago lawyer but also a financial consultant, who guided him to alternative sources of funding with which to continue farming. Even though his original reorganization plan was voted down by the Farm Credit System, he persevered, continuing to file monthly financial reports with the court, in effect buying time—vital for anyone who tried to stave off failure in the farm crisis—until the climate for negotiation improved. Eventually his patience was rewarded. The bankruptcy judge approved a revised plan, and this time the lenders were prepared to cooperate.

In sum, families, sometimes in consort with lawyers but often by themselves, showed that when pushed into a corner they were capable of looking after their rights in a manner that would have been beyond comprehension a few years before. At the same time it is important to emphasize that all those who chose to continue farming had to endure long uncertainty. Those over fifty were in an especially difficult position. They were more likely to suffer psychological trauma over failure and the potential loss of a farm, and their prospects of finding a job in the area were poor in the years 1984-1986. Unless their wives could find off-farm work, such families' prospects were grim.

Farm Activism

The stress and fear brought on by lender pressure and mistrust of the expensive and often poor service rendered by attorneys created what bankers called self-styled experts among farmers. These circuit-riding farmers or farm wives traveled the countryside to counsel others. Some had learned their tactics from outsiders, veterans of legal battles before the farm crisis even began in Iowa, who peddled ideas and literature of a dubious nature. The Iowa alumni of these "seminars," while sometimes subscribing to the ideas of the far right, were more interested in the nuts-and-bolts procedures required to save the farm of one of their "client's" than in a philosophy of hate based on conspiratorial theories as to why the farm economy was failing.[4]

One of the most active farmer advocates in northeast Iowa was in my sample. The eldest of four brothers in a clan who all farmed within a mile or so of each other, he had become a plunger in the seventies, expanding to over a thousand acres, bringing two sons into farming, and buying an interest in a grain elevator. In 1983 losses on the Board of Trade initiated actions by the Land Bank and a commercial bank to withdraw financial support. Under the threat of foreclosure, the father filed a Chapter 11.

For the next four years he fought his own battles against lenders and tried to assist others as well. This was a time of enormous strain and pressure for him and his family. His eldest son found the situation intolerable and left farming. And the farmer himself, under unremitting stress, acted unwisely.

Among other things the family was one of the few that went through Chapter 11 twice. The second was filed in 1986 after the farmer and his attorney discovered a loophole permitting another filing after all other routes to survival were blocked. In fact, this strategy was an indicator of the good relationship between the farmer and his bankruptcy attorney, who sometimes used him as a liaison with other farmer clients. The long period of living in bankruptcy made the man an expert in the art of frustrating efforts to repossess defaulted property. As an advocate he welcomed others who needed his advice. Farmers and their wives called for an appointment and came to his home when it was convenient. If they needed further assistance, he was prepared to accompany them to court to give moral support. Over these years he counseled scores of families on possible strategies to keep their farms in business. In 1986 he took mediation training and attended legal seminars to try to keep abreast of proposed changes in debtor law.

Not surprisingly, these activities caught the notice of the authorities. Whether his activism was a motive for the federal authorities to move against him is unclear. He told of visits of officials from the United States Department of Agriculture who wanted to know if he had taken payment for his advocacy services. What he had done was to sell sealed, mortgaged grain, a violation of the bankruptcy laws and the regulations of the Commodity Credit Corporation. The sale, an indictable offence, was the kind of mistake that many desperate farmers apparently contemplated but did not attempt for fear of getting caught. In this instance, speedy retribution followed. Prosecution and an indictment led to a federal trial in the spring of 1987. The farmer was convicted and sentenced to three concurrent two-year jail terms with all but thirty days suspended. The light sentence was partly the result of the intercession of character witnesses from the community.

The judge in his summation stressed that honesty and integrity were essential for the successful administration of any government grain program that depended on trust. "When the people across this district," he concluded, "understand that even the —— of this world have to face the music and face jail, this court hopes that the law will continue to be vindicated, and those who seek the protection of the bankruptcy court will feel obligated to abide by the law."[5]

In another area of the state a self-made man attempted to generate interest in community and statewide action to improve the sliding farm economy and to change the ways of intransigent lenders. This farmer was a plunger who had accumulated property in northern Iowa and as far away as Texas. A strong-willed Irishman, he railed against the farmers who "wouldn't stick their necks out," who were too intimidated to demand their legitimate rights. His own stumbling block was the high interest rates of the Land Bank; when he refused to make land payments after the increase, the agency foreclosed.

He worked to recruit community farmers to the National Farmers Organization as one method of raising prices, and he campaigned for profarmer candidates in the 1986 election, but he encountered only a frustrating lack of interest in his community. Finally he decided to publish an advertisement in the newspaper with the largest circulation in the state, calling for volunteers to take part in a class-action suit against the Land Bank and giving his name and home telephone number. Over a hundred farmers answered this call to action. At least some farmers were prepared to drop a "do nothing" approach and take the offensive.

Most farm communities had someone with a fair knowledge of agricultural law, and so after 1984 assistance was usually close at hand. In the rolling hills of western Iowa, women were preeminent in this role. One ran her own hotline without compensation and regularly accompanied families to mediation sessions, to court, or to lenders offices. What motivated the actions of advocates? To some extent they were spurred by a desire to make life as difficult as possible for institutions that they believed had wronged them without justification. Early on, anger certainly was a force in their actions. Later, the motivation came more from a desire to be useful to the community and to assist those overcome by a sense of hopelessness, who would otherwise have done little about their predicament.

Looking for Work

The conventional response to the loss of a job is to look for work elsewhere. The loss of a farm, however, is somewhat different from the elimination of an occupation in an urban environment. The farm is a home as well as a place of business. In addition, the middle-aged farmer with no other training and little education is at a disadvantage, compared to younger and better-prepared candidates for jobs.[6]

In actual fact, even though farm families were reluctant to move from their homesteads and jobs in most rural areas of Iowa were scarce, the evidence suggests that farmers and their families were remarkably adept at finding alternative sources of income in their immediate community.

Some research has suggested that distancing is an important element in any farm home in order to sustain an equilibrium among family members.[7] This was more important in the stressful environment created by the farm crisis. Thus when a family member took an off-farm job, the benefit was not only economic but psychological as well. Even a low-paying part-time job allowed the worker to escape the gloom of the home for a few hours.

The drive to obtain an off-farm job was often launched by the wife. Female employment in light industry, nursing homes, clerical work, or part-time, ill-paid service jobs was easier to obtain in small farm-related communities, than was male employment. In the seventies farm women usually had white-collar work of some kind, and others became active in small on-farm businesses. Craft shops and beauty salons were typical of the kind of self-employment opportunities available in these years. In the farm crisis, at least in the sample communities, farm women were most likely to find jobs in the service area.[8]

As in any job search the most satisfactory method of obtain-

Table 16. Financial Condition and Off-Farm Employment

| | Type of Job | | | | |
Financial Condition	None	Service	Labor	Prof	N
Worried about quitting farming	40.7%	40.7%	14.8%	3.7%	27
Under some pressure	46.8	31.9	8.5	12.8	47
Making a comfortable living	70.5	18.0	6.6	4.9	61
Total %	56.3	27.4	8.9	7.4	—
N	76	37	12	10	135

Chi Square = 12.4, p = .05

Table 17. Women's Off-Farm Employment

Financial Condition	No Job	Has Job	N
Worried about quitting farming	55.6%	44.4%	27
Under some pressure	55.3	44.7	47
Making a comfortable living	78.7	21.3	61
Total	65.9	34.1	135

Chi Square = 8.06, p = .01

Source: Sample Data

ing employment was through personal contact. Men used this strategy to obtain "traditional" jobs that could be had without relocation: laborer in a feed mill or elevator, truck driver, and mechanic. Other farmers gravitated toward janitorial and custodial work and school bus and mail route driving. Previous work experience and some kind of training and education obviously broadened the search.

As Table 16 shows, almost 44 percent of all families in the study had someone working off the farm full time. Those in the category "worried about quitting farming" were most likely to have off-farm jobs, and those "making a comfortable living" the least likely. Service occupations were favored, and a handful had laborers or professionals in the family. Over a third of all families had a female member employed in town. For women, however, the family's financial condition had less to do with the drive to secure employment (Table 17). Those families in greatest danger of leaving farming were no more likely to have a woman working than those "under some pressure." Even in families with few problems a fair proportion of women were working, reflecting not the farm crisis but a more general desire of women to get out of the home and go to work.

Few middle-aged men were willing to quit farming for a full-time occupation. One sample member did become a driver for a long-distance trucking firm and spent many weeks on the road away from the farm. Another worked as a mechanic for the railroad. A few went far in search of work, but the results were not encouraging. One husband went to Denver, rented an apartment, mailed out hundreds of resumés, but got no job offers. Six months later he returned to Iowa. Even children, whose age wasn't a liability, were frustrated by the vagaries of the economy in other areas of the country. One son moved to Oklahoma to work in a feedlot. He was replaced when his boss decided to cut expenses by hiring illegal aliens from Mexico for a dollar a day. He next got a job as a trucker for an oil company, only to lose it to the economic slump in the oil business. Some young people expressed their distaste for the Southwest and the burdens of living in sunbelt cities. Perhaps those who did not venture very far and scraped out a living in custom farm work showed a better understanding of the realities of the job market than the more adventurous.

Part of the state mobilization program was a job training scheme for farmers. Candidates were given psychological testing and attended interview and resumé-writing workshops. The program involved less job training than morale building among those who believed they had no skills to offer the world outside farming. Those sample families who attended seem to have gotten more confidence but no job prospects.

Those men with a college degree in a field like economics

had reasonable prospects of a job in some area that had expanded as a result of mobilization after the spring of 1985. One farmer was able to leave his operation in the hands of his son and father-in-law and go to work for the Farmers' Home Administration as a troubleshooter for the western Iowa offices. While he welcomed the opportunity to work, this job placed him on "the other side" from the farmer, and part of the job was to take abuse from distraught borrowers whose loans the FmHA was trying to terminate. Fortunately, about a year later a position in the state Department of Agriculture became available. This ex-farmer then became a grain inspector.

Women with teaching and nursing degrees were also able to put their training to good use. In several instances their ability to find a professional position was the difference between farm failure and remaining on the land.

Survivors

Inevitably the stress and strain of the downturn did disrupt some families. In northwest Iowa a farmer suffered losses in a local bank failure that eventually forced him into bankruptcy. A dispute with his lawyer over payment led to a bizarre episode in which the attorney claimed the farmer had threatened him. Rumors of this behavior found their way into the media and had an effect on his marriage. When interviewed he was living alone. His wife had left the farm for a home-care job in Sioux City. In northeast Iowa another family had limped along near bankruptcy long before the downturn began in earnest. By the winter of 1984-1985 they were on welfare, had had their electricity cut off, and were existing with no heat and light. Their eldest child was having severe problems in school; so his parents removed him. The father grew increasingly unstable in 1985. He and his son threatened a custom operator with a gun when the elevator that had financed his crop that year sent the operator out to harvest some of his fields. Somehow, the family was able to take advantage of the new farm program in 1986 and hang on one more year. But the wife left the husband in the fall, and it seemed likely that he would at last be forced to quit.

An extramarital affair caused a strange twist in the lives of one sample couple in 1986. Despite huge losses on an FmHA-funded operation, the father took a cavalier attitude toward his financial as well as his personal life. He moved out of the house and down the road to live with a younger woman. This behavior would not have been so remarkable, had not the woman also been his hog herder. Thus, every day the wife, sitting in the farmhouse, was forced to watch the pair arrive for work. At lunch they would leave, and two hours later return for evening chores, after which they left for the night.

Every so often the husband would come to the house and visit his younger children and perhaps take his wife out for the evening. These visits gave her hope that the marriage would return to some sort of equilibrium. Apparently she put up with this behavior because of the children and because, without any job skills, she believed that divorce would only make her situation worse. With the farm technically bankrupt, there was little hope for alimony or support payments for the children. Ironically two college-age children had derived some advantage from their parent's difficulties. They qualified for substantial scholarship assistance at small private liberal arts institutions that in normal circumstances the family could never have afforded.

Throughout the Iowa farm crisis, even with their backs to the wall, farm families grew enormously resourceful about preventing a catastrophe to their normal source of livelihood. No better measure of the determination of farmers to be independent even in adversity was their refusal to sign up for food stamps. Farm advocates worked hard in 1985 to make food stamps available to needy farmers and to publicize sign-up procedures, but the response continued to be lukewarm. Undoubtedly many were eligible, but stigma and pride held them back. The numbers indicate that even in July 1986 only 2,316, or roughly 2 percent of all farm families received food stamps; the average value of a payment was $179 per month. Yet the reluctance of farm families to seek this form of aid was in marked contrast to their wholesale use of the rest of the farm program.[9]

In general, then, those who got into trouble (in other words, who had to reorganize their business in some fashion) were skeptical of outside assistance. Whether by using the law to secure a measure of their rights, by seeking an off-farm job, or by using some other aspect of the mobilization effort, they determined to remain as independent as possible.

6

The Frugal Farmer

As one wag put it, for a farmer the definition of success in the eighties was still having part of what he possessed ten years before. Just under 60 percent of the families in this study did not "get into trouble," did not face foreclosure, give back land, file bankruptcy, or reorganize their operation. The selectivity of the crisis gave failure all the more sting. The sight of those who were relatively unscathed and able to take advantage of high livestock prices was just another humiliation for those who were forced to quit farming. Indeed, the corn-hog ratio (which is calculated by dividing the price of a bushel of corn into the cost of a hundred pounds of slaughter-ready hog) reached its all-time high in the summer of 1986, mainly because so many producers were forced out of livestock raising in 1983-1985, reducing livestock numbers greatly. In addition, the downturn brought the price of corn down. Thus, the resolution phase of the farm crisis was fraught with tensions just as the earlier phases had been. They were centered, however, not on whether the bank was going to foreclose but on whether a neighbor was going to take advantage of rock-bottom prices and buy up the tract lost in the downturn.

This chapter will explore not why some farms failed but why others, despite losses, remained relatively sound. The short answer is that those who weathered the crisis came from stable backgrounds, through which they had inherited property and credibility in their community; they remained diversified, had reasonably low debt, weighed major business decisions carefully, were enthusiastic about farming and unlikely to be drawn to outside distractions, had raised their children in the same mold as themselves to respect these values, and were blessed with some luck.

Certain of these qualities can be found in what some researchers have called the "independent" farm family. Such a

Table 18. Farming Style and Financial Condition, 1986

Financial Condition	Independent		Integrated	
	Percentage	Number	Percentage	Number
Worried about quitting farming	22.4	11	18.6	16
Under some financial pressure	20.4	10	43.0	37
Making a comfortable living	57.1	28	38.4	33

Source: Sample data; Chi Square = 7.2; p = .02.

family tends to resist "trends toward mechanization and larger farms," shows an "unwillingness to incur large debts" in the purchase of land and complex equipment, and thus steers away from the dependence on "outside services" such expansion creates. By way of contrast, the "integrated" farm family is eager to "adopt new scientific and technological methods" and accepts debt as a means of achieving a style of farming associated with expansion, mechanization, and a heavy reliance on purchased services.[1]

The sample farmers are classified by style of management and a financial condition in Table 18. Over half the "independent" farmers were making a comfortable living in the winter of 1986-1987, whereas most of the "integrated" farmers were in at least moderate trouble. Even so, the percentage of independent farmers worried about being forced to quit was greater than the percentage of integrated farmers in the same category. Still, the figures seem to indicate that a more conservative approach to farming was the secret to staying afloat in the farm crisis.

To some extent this was so, for expansion of an enterprise or the land base loomed large as a factor in failure. At the same time, the closely held farm corporations in the sample—incorporation was an important indicator of integration—were in better financial shape than other types of organization, such as family partnerships or sole proprietorships. Diversification was another key to stability in uncertain times and also an attribute of independence. The farms least likely to fail were the hog-dairy enterprises, the most diversified of all, whose practitioners traditionally worked the longest hours and were the most frugal in the way they farmed. On the other hand, other types of farms that were somewhat diversified (cattle-hogs, dairy, and hogs) showed only a slightly better financial position than grain farms, which were the least diversified enterprises.

Perhaps the relative worth of independent and integrated styles of management is best illustrated among cattle feeders, who not only farmed in a risky environment but also needed large amounts of equipment and financial backing to operate. Their specialization often precluded even taking advantage of a favorable grain market, for they fed most of their corn to livestock. Not surprisingly, they were in the worst financial shape of all the sample enterprises.[2]

In the final analysis, style of management, or farming philosophy, is probably easier to approach in qualitative than in quantitative terms, for no strong relationship was found between financial condition and farming style or family style. Rather, far and away the most important quantitative measures were inheritance (discussed later), and expansion.[3] The expansion of a particular enterprise—whether hogs, cattle, or dairy—required expensive equipment, new facilities, and very often more land. Iowa farmers rented and purchased blue Harvestores, put up hog-confinement buildings, and invested in new equipment during the seventies. Those who exercised restraint increased their chances of being in good financial shape after the worst of the farm crisis was over.

Farmers who resisted the temptation to expand were only too happy to expound at great length on the beauty of thrifty living. There were those who could say, "I never borrowed money to put a crop in," and, "We drove the car until it wore out." Some attributed their success to their upbringing. "I still have some of the old German teaching behind me," said one, or, "Daddy always said, 'If you can't pay for it you can't have it.' " One farmer felt sure that "if you can't make it with a quarter section, you can't make it anyway." Others insisted, "We always made sacrifices for good management." These farmers had learned many years before that farming provided relatively low returns, was subject to seasonal and cyclical trends, and every so often suffered spectacular booms and busts. They also knew, having had it drilled into them as youngsters, that farmers had to stick to long-term goals and not be sidetracked by the lure of quick and easy profits.

Farming as a Way of Life

One important question raised by the failure of so many progressive, or integrated, farm families is what their fall would do to agriculture as a whole? If large numbers of well-educated and innovative farmers failed, who would take their places in the future? Some of the case studies I present in this chapter should assist in answering this question. Surely the failure of so many farmers made the farm crisis a kind of watershed, a critical time when there could be rapid structural change in the corn belt that would possibly diminish the importance of the family farm and replace it with corporate farming.[4]

One of the secrets of successful family farming is the ability to balance the many competing demands on a farmer's time in order to come out ahead financially and, ultimately, to hand over the farm to the next generation. There is a danger that a farmer can become so absorbed in the task at hand that he neglects crucial chores that also need attention. During harvest, livestock often get short shrift, and paperwork and other management tasks are too easily shuffled to the side when something more pressing occurs outside. It is this unpredictability that has so far prevented a corporate takeover of agriculture. A staff-and-line model of organization, in which the manager sits in an office before a computer terminal and subordinates move the hogs, cart the manure, feed the cattle, and do all the rest of the dirty work, seems theoretically possible, but farming also has to deal with the weather and other vagaries of nature that make it inherently risky. Therefore, the giant food-production industry has preferred to leave the actual growing of food to farmers and to concentrate on the manufacture of finished products, which can be controlled with maximum efficiency. Until now corn-belt farming has never conformed to an ideal agribusiness formulation and retains many aspects of being a way of life rather than a business.

The ethic of hard work and simple living of the classic family farm is typified in the hog-dairy enterprise. The cows contribute the cash flow and the hogs, the profits—provided the family works from sunup to sundown. Ten families in the sample still made a living in this way, and all possessed a special dedication that made their farming style truly a way of life.[5] My first introduction to one of them came when I was driving down a country road in mid-June and saw a teenage boy mowing hay behind two Belgian horses. This family (the father and two grown sons were partners) milked sixty-five Holsteins, raised hogs, and bred Belgian draft horses as a hobby and for sale. On a dairy farm, horses could still perform such tasks as mowing and carting manure efficiently. Furthermore, the training for farm work enhanced the value of a work horse when it came to be sold. A trained two-year-old Belgian could fetch something in the region of three thousand dollars.

The parents were not native to the community. Rather, they had moved from central Iowa in the early sixties after a family dispute typical of that time. The wife, an Irish Catholic, had married her husband, a German Lutheran, much to the consternation of his parents. Because of this transgression, the prospects of farming in the home community vanished. Fortunately, a supportive banker friend helped them start out on their own. After renting a series of farms, they had moved to northeast Iowa.

A countrified facade disguised a shrewd and fairly cosmopolitan dairyman. As a board member of a milk cooperative he was conversant with the complexities of milk politics and government support programs. Trips to conventions in other parts of the country allowed him to meet other dairymen and to understand their problems. Probably his greatest ahievement, though, was to start two sons in farming in the seventies and early eighties without going bankrupt. Dairying, with its rigid and relentless schedule, is far removed from the three-month work year of the grain farmer. But provided the farm had not incurred too much debt, it was an ideal vehicle on which to ride out the downturn, especially if the farm raised hogs as well.

Regular milk checks made the banker happy. But even with a good cash flow, bringing children into farming made any operation vulnerable. Here, the father was able to use his judgment to guide the family through the dangerous period of 1983-1985. He managed to let some land he had bought a few years before go back to the contract holder before its value plunged. Likewise, he surrendered some machinery before much damage was done.

Both husband and wife were from the old school. They believed in driving their children, in making the teenage years a period of rigorous apprenticeship for farming. Indeed, one neighbor suggested that the trouble with "Tom" was that he made his children do all the work. But the sheet anchor of the family was the mother. A great trainer of children, she believed in the twin gospels of hard work and simple living. She confided that her eldest son, with whom she shared the barn duties, did not really have the temperament of a dairyman. His temper was awful, and she had tried for years to moderate his flare-ups. Reflecting on how change was altering life for the worse, she lamented that one of her daughters-in-law (a town girl) was incapable of running a household when she first got married. She could not cook and had apparently never done housework. Her mother-in-law did not want to interfere, knowing that she would have to work out this problem with her son. Her daughters, by contrast, made marvelous homemakers—thanks to her training—except that they never practiced these skills because they lived in distant cities and were always working.

Her own farm schedule centered on the dairy barn and hen house. Every morning and evening she milked the cows with her son and, like the farm wife of a bygone era, collected the eggs to sell to the neighbors. This routine was important to her. Once, she was forced to lay off after being crushed by a cow and suffering several broken ribs. Idleness had made her miserable, and she only recovered her spirits when she got back to work. Ironically in 1986 she got a job as a teacher's aide to earn a little money. Then it was her husband's turn to feel forlorn. For the first time in their life together the couple did not have each other's companionship throughout the day. This time he complained that everything was changing for the worse.

With the exodus of young men in their twenties from family

farms because of the downturn, how did this family manage to sustain three households on six hundred acres? As one son volunteered, there was no point in young people trying to farm in the eighties unless they were prepared to sacrifice. Both daughters-in-law worked, and the men were kept busy by the dairy, hogs, and horses. Apart from church and school activities, a few beers in the village on Saturday night was as much free time as was allowed. After a blistering day of haymaking, following the baler to pick up bales and toss them on the wagon, there was no break at all before milking.

But could frugality and professionalism go hand in hand? Was the entrepreneurial spirit snuffed out by all the failures of the "young tigers"? Could "hunkering down" act in partnership with a more aggressive modern approach to farming?[6] Perhaps these questions can be answered in part by looking at a northwest Iowa family whose farming style seemed to straddle the line between independence and integration.

A first meeting with this family furnished some classic insights into how an intergenerational farm family operates. Three generations were out in the field near one of their feedlots on a reasonably warm Sunday afternoon in November. The seventy-year-old parents, two of their sons, and a grandson were preparing to move some cattle from an enclosed feedlot to a paddock bordered only by an electric fence. The cattle, for whom this was a new experience, took fright. The electricity malfunctioned, and the cattle broke down the fence and wandered off to other areas of the farm. The next two and a half hours were spent repairing the fence and coaxing the cattle into their designated paddock. One would have thought the failure of the fence and the stupidity of the cattle might offer license to blow off steam with a few well-chosen words, but the family members appeared to take the stampede and the frustrations it generated for granted. Hardly a word was spoken. Indeed, no one seemed to be giving any orders at all in what turned out to be a fairly intricate operation. Patience, imperturbability, and seemingly telepathic powers of communication turned a major annoyance into routine.

The tradition of thoroughness and dedication to the job at hand blended well with the teachings of the land-grant college.

Both sons were graduates of Iowa State University and boosters of Extension Service ways. At the same time, with the younger especially, there was a frugal streak near the surface. A Marine officer in the Vietnam War, he took pride in demonstrating his thrifty life-style. He still drove a 1964 Pontiac, lived in a trailer with his baby son and wife, and plowed most of his money back into his pride and joy, his cattle-feeding operation. Since he spent four hours a day feeding the livestock, it was better, he said, to spend money for the Rolls Royce of dumpsters, which was used to load feed into wagons for transportation to the feed lots, than to throw away money on a flashy car. With a master's degree in animal husbandry, he was proficient enough not to require a veterinarian except in dire emergencies. He also gave record keeping great attention. Characteristically, though, he didn't use a computer; this man wouldn't waste funds on something for which paper and pencil were adequate. The records were a key to his management strategy. They told him everything he needed to know on the cattle enterprise on a daily basis: weight gain, cost of feed, as well as last month's and last year's figures for the same items. The good news and bad news were plain to see, and the records gave the necessary insights to make adjustments.

His brother was more gregarious, a natural leader in the community, a board member of a local bank, a former member of the Cooperative Extension staff, and an officer in the air force reserves. His resumé placed him in the front rank of Iowa farmers in their forties who would be called upon to give leadership in the post-crisis era of more limited horizons.

As was the case in most sibling partnerships, there were certain tensions and rivalries between the brothers. One specialized in cattle and was careful with his money; the other preferred hogs, and was a little more liberal with his spending. He had built himself a new home on one of the most pleasant acreages in the neighborhood. Huge trees towered over the spick-and-span house and farm buildings, which stood a little to the rear. It was the elder brother's involvement in extracurricular activities outside the family farm—his bank board activities and knowledge of agricultural finance and the limitations of farmer peers—that are of most concern here, however.

His was a position of some delicacy, for sometimes bank officers had to make decisions that had a direct and powerful impact on neighborhood farmers. The institution, which saw itself as a booster of community business activity, had taken on a number of risky loans that had been turned down by more conservative banks. By the fall of 1986 the bank had a high percentage of problem loans in its portfolio. There was a reshuffling of the staff, and a young troubleshooter president, who could not only placate the FDIC but also terminate as many of the problem loans as possible, was hired.

During this reorganization tensions were as high at the bank as they were on the surrounding farms. There was much discussion of strategy at board meetings. The elder brother suggested that the institution could solve its agricultural lending problems by making stringent record keeping a criterion for obtaining a loan or for continued support. His colleagues, fearing that the requirement would cause a mass exodus by those who were in reasonable financial shape, resisted this innovative idea. Nevertheless, his approach reflected the thinking of someone who believed that farmer performance over the past decade had been abysmal. So bad was the situation that it was necessary to begin a reeducation campaign to drive home the importance of accurate and comprehensive records in the farm business. Only through good records could the farm family properly analyze the strengths and weaknesses of its operation. Unfortunately experience showed that many farmers were not prepared to sit in front of a computer and use a spread sheet creatively; they had neither the education nor the temperament for such a management style. For years they had muddled along, cosseted by their lenders and government programs, refusing to learn new ways. Yet the elder brother's harsh assessment was tempered by an acknowledgment that most of his classmates at Iowa State evidently were not very proficient managers either, for only one or two were still farming.

Again the question should be asked, how did this particular family keep from faltering when so many of their neighbors fell? The answer in part was that they rested on the accumulated wealth of a hundred years of frugal living on the northwest Iowa prairie. In this instance, it was the maternal side that had longer

Table 19. Inheritance and Financial Condition, 1986-1987

	No Inheritance		Inheritance	
	Percentage	Number	Percentage	Number
Worried about quitting farming	32	18	12	9
Under some pressure	40	23	31	24
Making a comfortable living	28	16	58	45

Source: Sample data; Chi Square = 13.8; p = .001.

tenure: the family homestead was from this branch of the family. Their no-nonsense approach to farming had paid off in the seventies, when they made a substantial income. From accumulated capital they could self-finance expansion. They were able to purchase land and machinery without concern for the rise in interest rates. They had a cushion to ride out the bad times. Even so, they had taken a six-figure loss in the cattle enterprise only a few years before. But their cushion allowed the operation to hang on until 1986, when livestock prices again made their business profitable.

Inheritance

Farmers were very sensitive about the part inheritance played in their farming careers. One son when questioned about his father's estate plans reacted testily that they were none of his business. "In any case," he added, "I'll make all the money I need on my own." But the fact remains that he and many others in the sample received great assistance from familial and parental intervention. Inheritance—or rather, the lack of it—unquestionably contributed to the demise of some farms.

Clearly, as Table 19 shows, at the end of 1986 or in early 1987 families that had inherited were much better off than those that had not. Inheritance was defined as receiving property (most often land) through the auspices of the family. While the property might have been paid for with a contract from parents or transferred as a gift over a period of years in accordance with regulations, the important point to emphasize was that heirs had access to land they would eventually own through family contacts. In contrast noninheritors not only had to purchase land at commercial interest rates rather than preferential levels set by the family but also had to search for land to buy.[7] Obviously the family with a stable base had more financial and social advantages in the home community than one that moved in from elsewhere.

The failure of several farmers of large operations with a long tradition in one place who had received substantial assistance from parents indicated that those who seemed to hold all the advantages could also fall, through a combination of bad luck and poor management. Nevertheless, their demise masked the more general trend. Most of the intergenerational farms in trouble did not receive assistance through inheritance, and most of those in comfortable shape did. It could be said that inasmuch as all these farms were intergenerational, by definition the younger generation had received help to begin farming. Indeed, such assistance often got the farm into difficulties in the first place. However, there was a considerable difference between an expansion that relied entirely on borrowed capital and one in which some of the equity came from familial holdings accumulated over generations. Not surprisingly, it was common for those in less fortunate circumstances to observe that their debt-free neighbors were in a good position because they had been set up in farming by their parents. Only with Dad's help, then, did the fortunate survive.

The farm style and organization of inheritors were indistinguishable from those of the rest of the sample except in two important respects. First, as many as 92 percent of the closely held family corporations had inherited property. This was not surprising, for the very incorporation was symptomatic of a desire to avoid inheritance taxes and to keep the farm in the family. Second, those classified as professional farmers had a three-to-one chance of being inheritors, whereas conservatives, plungers, and middle-of-the-roaders had about an equal chance of being one.

All families were asked during the interview if they agreed with the statement "Farmers who used the inflationary climate of the late seventies and early eighties to expand deserve their fate." Although 57 percent of the sample disagreed with the statement, 44 percent of inheritors agreed. In other words, those who in some fashion owed their success on the farm to ascribed rather than achieved means were sometimes not especially sympathetic to the situation of those who had expanded and were then caught in the downturn. This is not to say that those with such views were callously indifferent to their neighbors' difficulties. As one remarked, "We don't like seeing friends in trouble." On the other hand, this man had little sympathy for those who were always "whining"; more often than not, he believed, their problems were caused by their own lack of judgment.

Inheritors who expanded enterprises, bought land, built farm buildings, or helped children begin farming outnumbered inheritors who did not. In this they behaved much like those who did not have their advantages. When inheritors expanded, often the crucial ingredient to their survival came from the legacy supplied by inheritance. For example, one of the families classified as professional had expanded its land base considerably and built a farrow-to-finish hog facility. None of this expansion would have been possible without help from their relatives. Their original farm was purchased by one set of parents, and their more recent purchases were partly financed by the wife's side of the family. They had left the PCA in 1983 because a local bank was offering a more favorable financing package, but by 1985 they were forced to renegotiate their loan. This process took a whole year to complete. According to the farmer, he was able to achieve a satisfactory outcome because of his negotiating skill, learned over many years as a member of the local school board. The infusion of more familial funds, combined with a satisfactory settlement on the amount of interest charged by the bank, allowed the family to continue farming with the same amount of flexibility (in what it could do with the borrowed money) that it had before.

The cushion of inheritance allowed another closely held

corporation to expand a cow-calf enterprise in the early eighties despite the objections of a nervous father. Because the expansion was self-financed or utilized private contracts, the sons were able to make suitable adjustments when the debt crisis materialized. Again, one large dairy partnership suffered heavy losses in an elevator failure. In 1984-1985 the operation was under pressure to liquidate a percentage of its property, but by 1986, thanks to a combination of better prices and a timely bailout from off-farm relatives, in the words of one of the wives, they "were never richer."

In another prominent family the sudden death of the head left his heirs in a quandary. His brother, who was a partner, had never concerned himself with management and financial issues, nor had the man's widow or daughters. Their rude awakening about the financial state of the business was followed by months of wrangling over how to place the operation on a sound footing. Land was sold, tenants ousted, and enterprises terminated in an effort to catch up on years of neglect and to conform with the lender's insistence on a lean and healthy farm. Despite every effort, there was some question that the task could be achieved without further loss, but the daughters planned their campaign of rehabilitation in the best tradition of the squirearchy. One of the pall bearers at their father's funeral was the president of the PCA, and they even invited their PCA loan officer to dinner on occasion. By 1987 many Iowa farmers who had dealings with the PCA had fled or been cut several years before. The idea of socializing with a lender, let alone one from the Farm Credit System, was anathema. However, in a well-established family, and especially one that had helped found the local PCA in the Depression, it seemed that the old courteous way of doing things still carried some weight.

Sometimes unexpected death only enhanced an already sound financial position. In the late seventies, one family inherited twelve thousand acres of rangeland in Wyoming from a cousin. This windfall permitted enormous expansion of their cow-calf operation in such a way as to make them independent of cattle dealers in the West. They were able to raise animals in Wyoming themselves and fatten them for market on their Iowa farms. When their bank failed in 1985, it was they who received a call from another institution inviting them to bring their account over. Another family, whose son said that they had never had a better year than 1986, had lost a mother a few years before. Her life insurance and her widower's remarriage to someone who brought property to the farm operation gave them ample leeway.

Young Farmers and Frugality

There were a number of young farmers in the sample who were surviving quite adequately in the farm crisis. Although they would not have been in this position without parental help in the first place, they disproved the notion that a whole generation of younger men was eliminated in the downturn. Not surprisingly, some were extremely conservative in their personal life. A few were "born again" Christians, who had a strong moral outlook on the need for thrifty living, the dangers of debt, and the importance of a rural setting for bringing up children. They had some justification in believing that their attitudes and style of farming had a certain validity after a decade of boom and bust.

One of these young farmers combined a number of unusual characteristics. He was a past president of the county Farm Bureau but also dedicated to self-sustainable agriculture. On his small self-financed farm he raised cattle and hogs, rotated crops, strip contoured, and refused to use chemicals. His strong views on alternative methods of farming were apparently self-taught and came from a desire to lead a better Christian life rather than through contact with farmers interested in operating without chemicals for ecological reasons. He and his wife claimed to have become "more conservative than ever" as a result of the farm crisis. Their major concern at the time of the interview was the amount of income tax they would have to pay for the year just passed.

Another ultraconservative young farmer, from a four-generation family of cattle feeders, had become a dairyman as if to prove his independence. The change was motivated partly by the return of an elder brother in the seventies after he had worked for a California supermarket chain. The dairyman was bitter that the prodigal son had returned to a full partnership in his father's operation. It was unfair. He himself had never been to college, having worked on the farm since leaving high school. What made his father's favoritism doubly hard to bear was that his brother's California-raised wife refused to live in the country and had to have an expensive home in town. As if in reaction to his brother's profligacy, he adopted an exaggeratedly frugal life-style. The only family activites off the farm involved the church. His wife, who had also come from an urban background, plunged into farm life with enthusiasm, as if to show up her sister-in-law.

Unfortunately, frugality did not necessarily have advantages in a world of unabated consumption. One son—who was nominated with his father as a hog producer of the year—lamented that he would probably never marry. None of the women he knew would think of marrying a farmer because of the risk and hard life. Such sentiments were echoed by a young wife who wanted her husband to quit his perfectly viable operation and move to the sun belt.

Even without the pressures of the downturn, young farmers in an intergenerational operation had to deal with the problems of blending into a family business full-time. In some instances the older generation was very rigid in the way it ran things, and the farm crisis served to reinforce this bedrock conservatism. The dairyman who got up every morning at five o'clock and drove his manure spreader through the village to his fields, was concerned in the early eighties that his sons were not prepared to tolerate this kind of regimen and none of them would succeed him. This worry increased when his health deteriorated. Fortunately, his youngest son, who had not seemed to have the patience to become a dairyman, suddenly blossomed into an enthusiast. The father, who never allowed anyone to touch his cows and who vacuumed their coats once a week, glowed with pride over the husbandry of the young man and his apparent willingness not only to enroll in this difficult apprenticeship program but to thrive under a rigorous taskmaster.

On one hog-dairy farm strict paternalism in intergenerational relations mixed with a degree of entrepreneurship unusual for this type of operation. The family raised exotic animals (bison, deer, and a variety of birds) as well as the full complement of farm livestock. The family seed-corn business had suffered a few delinquent accounts, but on the whole they were hardly affected by the downturn. The farmstead was isolated from the nearest village and had become a gathering place for the neighborhood. At all times of the day gossip and coffee were liberally dispensed by the family head and his son. Despite this air of bonhomie, the father ruled like a patriarch over the operation, ignoring his son's willingness and obvious ability to be given more responsibility. As it had his grandfather in the Depression, debt "scared him to death," and he felt that in the risky economic climate it was a bad time to change leadership. Therefore, he determined not to allow management out of his hands. After all "the kids and hired men depend on me," he said.

Not all young farmers were frustrated by the recalcitrance of their elders. One man's father lent him forty thousand dollars with which to settle his divorce after his first marriage failed. He had entered farming when a career in farm journalism went awry and had secured Farmers' Home Administration loans to begin to raise hogs. His early years were not easy. By trial and error he had become a competent hog producer, although a fire had destroyed one of his barns, his hogs had suffered from bloody scours, and he had only just managed to persuade the bank to convert his short-term loan to one guaranteed by the FmHA. After he survived these trials, the farm crisis held few terrors, and he had a felicitous outlook on life.

While the farm crisis dealt serious blows to the farm careers of some young men and often stifled initiative, for some it did provide opportunities. To one financially secure sample member it gave the necessary motivation to run for public office. A thoughtful and articulate spokesman for cattle raisers, he thought the very act of running would stimulate a useful discussion of the renaissance of agriculture. But he had little chance in the Republican primary against the party's handpicked candidate. Obviously the initiative of this young farmer was not strangled by the farm crisis, nor was it for the son of another sample member, who, at this father's insistence, made all financial, marketing, and farm program decisions, while his father continued to perform the heavy field and livestock work.

There is little doubt, then, that the fear of losing a whole generation of young farmers to the downturn did not materialize.

Ironically, the farm crisis reaffirmed the cultural traits of generations of corn-belt families. What is called the yeoman style of farm management and family organization—continuity, risk-aversive financial practices, the limitation of expansion to fit family needs, intergenerational succession, and cooperation—which had guided families through a century of economic uncertainty in corn-belt agriculture, still applied. When others had adopted the new entrepreneurial style of farming championed by agribusiness and the land–grant colleges, in which risk taking, specialization, and above all capital were given a high priority, the yeoman remained true to the frugal principles that had stood him in good stead for so long.[8] For Iowa farm families the most visible lesson of the farm crisis was the reminder that corn-belt farming rewarded those with a long-term commitment to the land, those who worked to hand over the farm to the next generation. The passion of the 1970s for specialization fell short where diversification succeeded.

7

Retrospect and Prospect

Not surprisingly, rapid change had an impact on the infrastructure and the people who lived and worked in farm communities. But given the magnitude of the transformation and the many underlying problems that beset agriculture, one of the most striking aspects of these years was the lack of debate among farmers themselves as to the future of family farming. To be sure, on the sidelines there was no lack of discussion between factions claiming to represent the farmers. But in general it seemed, to use a sporting analogy, that the farmer-players ran round the field in a daze while the crowd shouted itself hoarse in an effort to influence the outcome. The time was ripe for a thorough overhaul of agricultural policy, but it would seem that the more things changed on the farm, the more they stayed the same with the farm program.

The unwieldy and expensive support of farmers through government commodity loans and deficiency payments is the key to understanding the passivity of the majority of farmers. After 1982 the feed grain program acted as a safety net for many operations. Because there was no limitation on their distribution, larger farmers and the grain trade (through Commodity Credit Corporation storage fees) reaped the greatest benefits. The corn farmer who received an average of $2,282 in 1983 made $5,520 in 1985. Considering the costs involved to produce a crop, this was hardly a windfall.[1] However, aggregate figures put government payments in a different light. As much as $10.5 billion went to corn producers as a whole, and $25.8 billion to the total farm program in 1986.

At the individual level, then, the 1985 Farm Bill provided the farm family with a known quantity. In a world undergoing transformation the program remained reassuringly the same. For this reason, 60 percent of all Iowa farmers in the spring of 1987 said they were in favor of retaining most of the provisions of the bill. Since lenders and agribusinessmen also had everything to gain and little to lose from this priming of the pump by the federal government, alternative solutions had little chance of success.[2]

As I suggested at the outset of this book, a number of themes played important roles in the evolution of the Iowa farm crisis. Three of these—lender-farmer confrontation, farm advocacy, and media coverage—have received considerable attention elsewhere and will be treated only briefly here. The fourth theme, government programs, requires lengthier discussion. First, however, it is important to note the issues brought up in the debate over the future of the family farm by farmer advocates, members of the agricultural establishment, and other observers of rural America, before attempting to draw some conclusions about the events of the past decade in the Iowa countryside and their effect on the farm family and rural social structure.

The Debate over the Family Farm

During the farm crisis rural America was subjected to a common phenomenon of modern life, extensive coverage by the electronic media. Some attention was beneficial in exposing the problems of failing farmers, but rarely did the news media have the time to explore the intricacies and ironies of the downturn. The public lacked a good deal of information about what was happening on the farms and in the small towns. Even the farm families themselves, engaged as many of them were with the day-to-day struggle to keep their farms afloat, preferred to let the agricultural establishment, the newer farm advocate groups, and other experts debate farm policy issues.

The record would suggest that the neopopulist farm advocates from groups allied to the Iowa Farm Unity Coalition won the battle over electronic media coverage with their skillful courting of television and the press early in the farm crisis. On the other hand, they were less successful in the more important contest over the farm bill, which they wanted to use as a vehicle to begin to transform agriculture. The public relations campaign to highlight the farm problem was so satisfactory that it tended to exaggerate the plight of farmers. An exchange taken from a panel discussion on the future of American agriculture tackles the question of media intrusion and influence from the perspective of one of the interested parties, the establishment. During the discussion the moderator made this observation:

Last year we had a wave of media attention to the "farm crisis" in which one basic story was told: Farmers are going broke. You saw it over and over on network television, Time magazine, you saw it in movies, "Country," and others. It seems to me the media wave, like all media waves, dissipated on the shore somewhere in 1986 and it's more quiet.

Panelist: Plus the fact that it wasn't really happening. It wasn't really true.

Moderator: It wasn't true?

Panelist: It wasn't true. It had a grain of truth. How many farmers have we lost? How many farmers have not gotten credit like everybody said they weren't going to? It was overblown, and I think we've got a credibility problem.[3]

For the establishment and for one of its spokesmen, an agricultural economist, the farm crisis was a technical problem to be solved scientifically. The media, by concentrating on the human side of the story and emphasizing the trauma of confrontation with lenders and the dislocation of families, ignored the complex economic aspects of the downturn. The "cancer" of high interest rates, for instance, had far more to do with the continued crisis than the intransigence of bankers. Again the capacity of farmers to recycle, to stay on in the community and start farming again, refuted the image of the forcible eviction and the wholesale exodus of yeoman farmers.

The cornerstone of the neopopulist response to the problems of rural America was the "Save the Family Farm Act," which would have imposed mandatory controls on production and the amount of land that could be farmed. Its basic objective was to raise farm prices through a modest increase to the consumer in the price of food. Neopopulists envisioned an economy in which the ideal unit of production was the family-sized farm. The farm crisis had demonstrated to them the absurdity of a system based on the economic relationships of the seventies, and the "Save the Family Farm Act" aimed to provide an alternative. Its cornerstone, the minimum-price provision, was offered as the equivalent of the minimum wage in urban occupations. The neopopulist program also had other important aspects, notably a concern for the future of land tenure, the initiation of refinancing provisions for farmers, and the reorganization of the principal lender to agriculture, the Farm Credit System.[4]

The question of structural change in the countryside, especially the issue of who would control farming if the status quo were allowed to continue, was a major concern of neopopulists and provided a rhetorical flourish to the debate. The issue was well articulated by one leading spokesman, who wrote, "The skewed concentration of control over land and food production reinforces the development of a feudal system of land ownership and tenant farming." If things continued unchanged, Iowa would come to resemble Central America. Policy and opinion makers, he went on, seldom confront "the gross disparities of power and wealth" he found so apparent in the countryside. In this respect, both political parties "represent and articulate the desires of the powerful, while the needs of the dispossessed go largely unmet." It was time to decide "whether we are willing to stake out our claim of solidarity with those who may be dispossessed and to what degree we allow the powerful to define our lives."[5]

This rhetoric, though quite appropriate for a talk to a collective farm in Nicaragua, had some limitations when it was offered to an audience of Iowa farmers. At the grass-roots level, though farmers recognized that they were manipulated by agribusiness and government controls, they did not think of themselves as downtrodden or dispossessed. Indeed, they probably identified themselves more with the critical observations of neoconservative commentators who also took the measure of rural America in the farm crisis.[6]

For instance, one widely read article, which appeared at the low point of the downturn, gave urban America a quick update on the farm problem. The author listed eleven "widely held misconceptions" about agriculture. Contrary to media coverage, he wrote, most farmers were not poor, they were not being driven off the land, agribusiness did not dominate farming, and most farmers did not get subsidies. The writer, who had toured Iowa in

the winter of 1985, then went on to criticize some farmers for
their high standard of living while dependent on FmHA loans.
As an alternative to this welfare agriculture he offered the giant
Harris farms enterprise in California as an example of a successful operation without government assistance.[7]

Neoconservatives were indifferent to the romantic image of
the family farm. If neopopulists wanted to promote the "Save the
Family Farm Act" to preserve farming as a way of life in a
"Jeffersonian countryside of small independent landowners,"
one critic wrote, it was too late. That world had disappeared.
Farmers were little different from other segments of society. They
wanted to make money and live better than their parents.
"Urbanites often confuse the folksy ways of some farmers with
an indifference to material wealth," he went on. "The differences
between farmers and city-dwellers lie not in a different attitude
towards money, but in different choices about what to spend it
on." While the average lawyer wants money to buy a BMW, the
average farmer "may prefer a big pick-up truck with floodlights
and a motor home."[8]

According to the neoconservative lexicon, family ownership
of farms was not in danger from large organizations, for the
monetary return on farm operations was too insignificant for
giant corporations. Family farming was alive and well, but its
composition was dramatically different. It was now divided into
five classes: rural residences (hobby farms), small family, family,
large family, and very large farms. Small farms depended on off-
farm work for most of their income, and large farms had enough
resources to survive; it was those in the middle, those big enough
to require full-time work but not big enough to take advantage of
new technology, that were vulnerable. These were the primary
target of the "Save the Family Farm Act."

These farms, which on average had assets approaching $1
million, had outlived their time. Their operators got paid only
when they sold a crop. In between harvests they actually had to
borrow money to live on. Only in farming did someone need to
take out a loan to keep a job. Not only were medium-sized
farmers at the mercy of interest rates, the weather, and the markets, they also found themselves in one of the most dangerous
occupations. In addition, in order to achieve efficiency they had

to submit to a "draconian" work schedule in which self-exploitation and the exploitation of children were accepted practices. Perhaps farmers themselves had the last word on the viability of the family farm, for while farm programs had come and gone, they, and especially their children, continued to leave the land.[9]

This example of the "hip" journalism of the late eighties was principally aimed at deflating the romantic image of the family farm. To a degree some of the rhetoric could be substantiated. Take the important question of the exodus from farming and whether it was caused by push or pull. The defiant yeoman meeting the sheriff at the farm gate was as much a symbol of unwillingness to face structural change as a token of the desire to protest the methods of lenders. It is interesting to speculate what would have happened in Iowa if farm advocacy had not become as strong as it did. The assumption was that farmers wanted to stay on their land, that they supported the fight to save family farms, but there is some evidence in my sample to show that this was not necessarily so. The miserable job prospects for males over forty-five probably had as much to do with many decisions to remain on the farm as any belief in the sanctity of a century-old farm. The few farmers in the sample who did leave and obtained an off-farm job expressed relief, and even joy, that they were free at last from the stress of operating under the intolerable gaze of the lender. Farmers under fifty who had no particular financial concerns and whose families had farmed for several generations often seemed less than militant in defending their right to farm at all costs. Some had wives with salable skills in nursing or teaching. They had friends in urban occupations and living in other areas of the country who had none of the frustrations of farming in the eighties. Although none had done so, they discussed the option of leaving farming and relocating far from Iowa. Perhaps the most damning slight of agriculture was that so few of their children intended to follow them as guardians of a hundred-year tradition.

One example will illustrate this point. I reinterviewed one sample member in the winter of 1987, when he was under severe pressure from the Land Bank. His family had farmed in the neighborhood for well over a hundred years. The farm was located in some of the most picturesque country in the state, although the hills and woods did not make for very productive agriculture. In an interview in 1985 the conversation had turned to the relative difficulty of making a living on such land. The farmer intimated that despite the drawbacks, he would not exchange the river, the valley, and the woods for even a section of the black-earthed prairie of central Iowa. It was for this natural beauty that his ancestors had come to the neighborhood in the 1850s and for this that he was going to remain.

Two years later, he and his brother had decided to quit. They had sold their livestock, and while they waited for a decision from the lender's lawyers, they spent every day at the local commodity broker watching the markets on the satellite television. Their response to the pressure from the Land Bank, which refused to negotiate on a forty-acre parcel, hardly fit the stereotype of the defiant yeoman. Both determined to leave farming— "a horrible life," one bluntly called it. "Our families," the other said, "will never have another child in farming."

If farmers themselves may or may not have wished to save the family farm, in the iconography of Americana its image still carried great weight. Mainstream farm organizations cited it to justify their continuous quest for a bloated and wasteful farm program, and farm advocates used it to portray the farmer as a member of the downtrodden yeomanry, helpless under the boot of heartless capitalism. In a real sense saving the family farm became a platitude useful to a variety of individuals and organizations. Contrary to the claims of the neopopulists, both Republican and Democratic politicians used the issue for all it was worth in their election campaigns in Iowa. In the senate race in 1986, the Democratic candidate, in his professional capacity as an attorney, was involved in a class-action suit against the Farm Credit System. His opponent, the incumbent, took on the same agency in 1985 in a series of congressional committee hearings. The change in attitude of the Farm Bureau from 1984 and 1985, when it trumpeted its "free market" rhetoric, to 1987, when it endorsed a so-called decoupling plan that would pay farmers for not planting crops, underlined a willingness to forgo principle for expediency's sake.

The farm families in the middle found little of value in all this verbiage packaged for their consumption. The agribusiness gospel espoused by technicians was found wanting. Exhortations to keep better records and to diversify did not sit well with those who had heard a different message ten years before: that leveraging was the answer to inflation. Similarly, most farmers felt uneasy with the neopopulist vision of rural America. Not surprisingly, farmers became more cynical and alienated than ever before in a world where only the farm program seemed to provide a lifeline.

The Salience of Farm Programs

Most farmers interviewed disliked farm programs. They wanted to be independent and they found the red tape bothersome. Traditionally, most Iowa farmers fed much of their grain to their livestock rather than take it to market. However, in the eighties participation, even for livestock producers, became virtually mandatory to stay solvent. The tool most often used to cut production was the acreage set-aside provision. At the farm level—human nature being what it is—farmers took their least fertile acres out of production. And since there was nothing in the regulations to prevent them from increasing production on the land that remained with crops not affected by the set-aside, this is invariably what occurred. Such practices were fairly common in the eighties, and particularly during the payment-in-kind year of 1983.

The manipulative side of farming and agribusiness does not sit well with the romantic image of the family farmer, but in an environment where production, rather than stewardship, received so much attention, where land was just another commodity to be bought and sold, and where it paid to obtain maximum yields in a market already awash with grain, such behavior was often more prevalent than some were prepared to admit. As in other occupations, values began to change. Once the farm crisis hit there was a further acceleration. "It used to be in agriculture—and still is for the vast majority—that your word is your bond," said one observer. "But there are now increasing numbers of farmers where maybe this isn't the case. This doesn't mean that they are any more dishonest than anybody else, . . . but sometimes your concepts change."[10]

This change in morality was for years aided and abetted by government intrusion. The worst aspect of the farm program, like the income tax, was that it provided temptation for abuse. The tax code for farmers encouraged them to take advantage of investment tax credits. As a result, so ingrained was the attitude that they had to "beat the taxman" with deductions that sometimes farmers made questionable end-of-year purchases that later caused them difficulty. A good many expensive tractors sold at farm sales during the downturn had been purchased for this very reason. The intrusion of high-tech gadgetry into farmers' lives allowed them instant access to the financial markets, the Board of Trade and the Chicago Mercantile Exchange. The increased visibility of hedging and commodity trading encouraged their use by farmers. But commodity trading, dominated by large institutions, was a dangerous area to enter, the downfall of the unwary. One of the most incongruous sights I witnessed while interviewing families was in the kitchen of a farmer whose background and indeed style of operating in the field was classically "yeoman" in orientation. Sitting down to a meal, the family left the commodity market screen on. The head of the household said grace and crossed himself, all the while watching the numbers dancing across the television screen.[11]

In the area of government programs nothing personified the new "culture" of the high-tech agribusinessman quite as well as the payment-in-kind generic certificate in 1986, with which a farmer could make more money on a paper transaction than working in the field. Briefly, the feed grain program of 1985 had two components: deficiency payments and commodity loans. The latter were loans of up to $1.92 per bushel of corn after it was harvested. A farmer could sell his grain and pay back the loan or keep the loan and forfeit the grain to the government. In a glutted market, of course, virtually all would forfeit. Deficiency payments were direct payments to support farm income when market prices were below a certain target set by the government. The target price for corn in 1986 was $3.03 a bushel—arrived at through a combination of loan and deficiency payments. Farmers could obtain this target price only by idling 20 percent of their corn acreage. Direct payments had two components—cash and the payment-in-kind certificate—which added up to $1.11

per bushel of corn. In 1986 the regulations stipulated that a farmer could receive no more than fifty thousand dollars for the first, 63-cent portion of his deficiency payment. This payment was calculated from a formula multiplying a farmer's planted acres by his established corn yield and multiplying the product by his deficiency payment.

In both the short term and the long term, payment-in-kind certificates were meant to solve the problem of huge surpluses. In the long term they were to be used in conjunction with the Conservation Reserve Program (a new version of the old Depression set-aside program), which aimed at withdrawing millions of highly erodible acres from production. In Iowa a total of 1.4 million acres were in the program by 1987. Farmers agreed to keep this land out of production for ten years and to plant it with trees or permanent cover crops. The program paid them an average of seventy-seven dollars per year for each acre set aside. At the same time they received so-called corn bonus payments in payment-in-kind certificates amounting to two dollars per bushel for the corn they would have planted in 1987.[12]

In the short term the PIK certificate was meant to keep the grain market moving at a time of glut. With prices so low, it was logical that farmers would forfeit corn rather than pay back their loans. For this reason the USDA decided that a farmer could take out a loan and technically store his grain as collateral. However, rather than keep the grain in storage for nine months, as was the custom, he could immediately redeem the crop with PIK certificates, which were either issued to him or bought on the open market. The practice that came to be known as "PIK and ROLL" was based on the idea that a quick profit could be made if the farmer redeemed his corn not at the high loan rate but at the lower local cash price.

The process worked as follows: a farmer sealed his corn at the government rate of, say, $1.85 a bushel and received this amount in cash. He then turned around and bought enough certificates to cover all the corn he had in storage. The posted price of corn locally was, for example, only $1.29 a bushel. Since a PIK certificate was worth 120 percent of its face value at this time, the farmer had had to pay $1.55 a bushel for his certificates—the $1.29 cash price plus the 20 percent differential. The farmer could then immediately "roll over" the certificates, that is, turn them in to the government as repayment for his commodity loan. He could then redeem the crop that he had technically put in storage a few minutes earlier. The key to quick profits came here: the farmer paid back his loan of $1.85 with a certificate worth $1.55 per bushel and so made an instant profit of 30 cents per bushel. The beauty of PIK and ROLL was that the farmer still owned the corn and could then sell it at market prices. Such a scheme fitted perfectly into the climate of the late 1980s, when stock manipulation became an art. Not unexpectedly, the designers of PIK and ROLL quickly left their posts at the USDA for positions with large grain companies.[13]

It goes without saying that PIK and ROLL was hardly planned with the family farm in mind, as the complexities in my explanation testify. The program further enhanced the notion that USDA was run in partnership with and often as a handmaiden to agribusiness. For the ordinary farmer, while participation in the farm program was a necessity, it often seemed almost more trouble than it was worth. After stories began to appear in the press in the summer of 1986 about client abuse of the program, the government reacted by hiring a bigger staff at each office and computerizing records. Sample members reported stringent procedures by the Agricultural Stabilization and Conservation Service staff to keep abuse to a minimum. Amazingly, the rules for participation were biased in favor of just those groups of farmers that deserved the program least. For instance, the so-called corn base of farmers who traditionally were livestock producers was lower than that of those who had always emphasized grain farming and had typically ignored crop rotation in their fields. Thus a family that had been a good steward of the land for many years was at a disadvantage in the program compared to those who had exploited it.

Similarly deficiency payments were calculated in a way that worked against the family farm with corporate shareholders or family partners. One family could receive no more than $50,000 for the first, sixty-three-cent portion of the deficiency payment. Thus if a sixty-three-cent share amounted to, say, $85,000—a reasonable figure for some of the farms in the sample—they could receive only $50,000. But if several unrelated individuals established a joint venture in which each of them acted as an independent partner and controlled his or her own interest, each was eligible for the maximum payment.[14]

In Iowa where there were smaller farms and strict rule enforcement, there was less incentive to put forth the cost and effort to sidestep the regulation, and so there was less abuse. Only 13 percent of the sample could be classified as major users of the farm program. Several bitterly complained of the unfairness of regulations, noting that their legitimate family operations were being penalized while others had clubbed together to form partnerships of convenience to take advantage of the program. Because of the restrictions, the paper work was enormous. One farmer found the red tape so frustrating that he admitted he favored mandatory controls rather than submit to another round of the 1985 program as it was constituted.

Others, who were more oriented to accountant-style farming, welcomed the farm program and treated it as just another business opportunity. In one sample county a farmer who also ran a real estate business and farm-management company formed two partnerships, which gleaned $134,000 and $90,000 from the farm program, respectively. He and his partners were able to take advantage of the large inventory of land held by the Farm Credit System and other lenders. These properties were custom farmed by young men who had fallen in the farm crisis. One, a sample member, had rented over three thousand acres and purchased thousands of dollars' worth of machinery in the early eighties, without, he claimed, ever intending to pay full price for it. He planned to sell the equipment and buy more with inflationary dollars. Using eager salesmen and gullible loan officers to finance machinery purchases and operating loans, he had pyramided one loan on top of another until the house of cards collapsed in 1985. His lenders were so lax in their supervision that they had trouble piecing together an inventory of machinery and rental agreements. While the young farmer landed on his feet, the bank took a heavy loss.

For some, then, government intervention was an invitation to move agriculture farther along the route toward the value system of mainstream business. In the words of one respondent, in the ruthless world outside farming, it was a case of "dog eat dog" to stay alive.

For the majority there was an ambiguous relationship between family farmers and a farm program designed by businessmen. The introduction of the PIK certificate as part of the governmental effort to move grain gave the program the flavor of a lottery. At the same time, the Conservation Reserve segment seemed to have some merit, for it at least began to deal with the erosion problem on many farms and took millions of acres out of production.

Unfortunately, families got used to the infusion of funds from the government, regardless of the inconvenience it caused. The flow of federal funds into checking accounts began to be taken for granted, and many farmers found the weaning from government programs most difficult.

Control of the Countryside

It is necessary to ask what effect the farm crisis had on land tenure and the farm family (particularly the intergenerational farm) as an institution. For the control of landownership remains the most fundamental issue in a rural environment, and the future of the family farm depends on it. The long history of debate about who will own the land can be judged from the arguments of farm advocates in the 1970s and 1980s who harked back to the ideas Thomas Jefferson held two hundred years before. Did the reality correspond to the rhetoric?

It is worth noting at the outset that trends in the structure of tenure occur slowly and are changeable and unpredictable. As late as 1939, for example, almost 12 percent of all Iowa land was in corporate hands as a result of the Depression. Seven years later banks and insurance companies had once again surrendered ownership to the family farmer. To predict the future would be foolish. Rather, it is worth emphasizing some known emerging trends that at least have some basis in fact. I have already mentioned the essential economic rationality of the family farm in the corn-belt setting. The warnings of farm advocates about the "Central Americanization" of corn-belt agriculture were largely bluster. Actually, there was little danger that Iowa would be colonized and exploited by corporate interests, partly because of the work done by advocates themselves. Farm advocates successfully lobbied for restrictions on corporate ownership both before and during the farm crisis. In the middle seventies Iowa passed an anti-corporate-ownership law, which permitted limited partnerships and groups of investors but restricted corporate ownership to closely held family corporations. In 1987 this law was further strengthened by limiting partnerships of investors to fifteen hundred acres of land. Those with greater amounts were allowed to retain ownership provided they leased the land back to previous owners.

To be sure by the spring of 1987 patterns of landownership in Iowa were in a state of flux. Agencies such as the Farmers' Home Administration had control of sixty-four thousand acres of land repossessed from farmers. The Farm Credit System reported that it had sold 804 farms totaling ninety-three thousand acres in the first three months of the year. The system claimed that these farms were being bought by local farmers and by residents of the area in which the land was located.[15] Obviously discovering who was buying farmland valued at depressed prices would require a massive research effort over an extended period of time—something well beyond the scope of this study—but there is enough spotty evidence to suggest certain trends.

The ability of investors to take advantage of the vulnerability of the family farmer and become a major force in the land tenure of Iowa is the first question to examine. Historical evidence shows that absentee farm owners generally had an enviable record in regard to their investment. A study of five hundred absentee owners mainly in midwestern states such as Iowa, Indiana, and Illinois in 1984 showed that most lived within twenty miles of their land. As many as 48 percent were retired, and there were many ex-farmers in the ranks. In all, 50 percent had inherited their land, and most intended to keep it in the family. Although 64 percent of these farms were operated by tenants, there was a record of stability in this tenure. A total of 15 percent had farmed the land for twenty years or more, and another 58 percent had farmed the same land for six to twenty years.[16] On the other hand, a more recent survey of Minnesota in

1986 during the farm crisis pointed to the highest level of activity by investors since the 1960s. They represented 17 percent of all purchasers of farmland in the state. At the same time, farmers who already owned land nearby and desired to increase their holdings, constituted 72 percent of all purchasers, just as they had a decade before. The rural real estate market remained localized in Minnesota. Buyers living within five miles of a tract made up 46 percent of all those in the market, and 71 percent lived within ten miles.[17]

It is doubtful that Iowa patterns were much different. The mistrust of "outside investors" was well established, as the real estate industry was only too aware. "Let's face it," said a developer interested in buying foreclosed Land Bank property. "If a bunch of Jewish guys from Beverly Hills come in with a $100 million and start buying farms, they are not going to be well received."[18] In the hard-hit northern grain area investor purchases were publicized, but a perusal of the deed books of one county in the study area for 1986-1987 showed that local purchases still dominated the inventory of sales. Where investors were active, they had ties with the neighborhood. In Grundy County, usually recognized as having some of the best land in the state, out of thirty sales, eleven pieces of property were bought by outsiders and another eleven were purchased by active farmers. On the other hand, "nonfarmers" apparently bought 70 percent of the acreage sold.[19]

If investors were playing a greater role as landlords, what of their tenants? Because of the high price of land in the seventies, renting became more and more common. The median number of acres rented by sample members in this study was 220, and it was not uncommon for them to pay over $150 an acre cash rent for the privilege of working their landlord's farm. With the downturn, the scramble for rental land continued. Not only could a tenant participate in farm program payments on rental land, but renting freed a tenant from the expensive tax and maintenance obligations of ownership when money was tight. In addition, for the first time since the Depression, share renting came back into fashion, because it eliminated the need for cash. Under this system landlord and tenant shared the costs and profits of a crop.[20]

These changes in rental arrangements and increases in the number of renters who farmed the land of absentee landlords had ramifications for families. Much of the risk was carried by the landlord, and the farm family that rented could avoid crippling losses in land values and commodity prices. A handful of families in the sample were in this position. One had lived on an absentee-owned farm—a legacy of the Depression—for two generations. Two brothers in their thirties worked several farms owned by a family in the paint business in Cedar Rapids, which had bought the land after failures in the 1930s and rented it to the same family ever since. For all intents and purposes this was a very satisfactory arrangement. Relations between landlord and tenant were good; indeed they socialized together throughout the year. In the boom the business arrangement between them was based on shares. When the cattle enterprise lost money, the landlord decided to liquidate and concentrate entirely on hogs. Another family rented a farm from a local Lutheran church, which had been given the property in trust at the death of a member. A metropolitan bank had administered the land since 1955. Again the relationship seemed to work well: large capital improvements were the landlord's responsibility; the tenant paid cash rent for the land and raised livestock on fifty-fifty shares.

These long-standing rental arrangements with benevolent absentee landlords may prefigure a possible trend. The evidence suggests that investors were as likely to come from those with ties to a community—for example, those who were born in an area but moved away to urban centers after college—as from outside it. Such people were often altruistic in their motives: they wanted to do something for their native community. By buying land they hoped to keep it in the hands of those with local ties, thwarting total outsiders. Though these owners did not farm the land themselves, they rented it to neighborhood farmers who benefited from the local control of the land.

The key to control of the countryside would seem to depend on the resiliency of the family farm. Nervousness over the future of the countryside ignores the basic strength and organization of this institution, and especially the importance of intergenerational cooperation. The farm crisis revived the economic functions of the extended family. Farmers relearned the importance of sharing resources, and all forms of assistance between generations experienced renewal.

Such an interpretation suggests the value of considering change in cultural terms. Building on previous work, in which I looked at the behavior of Iowa farm families through a historical perspective, this cultural interpretation confirms the earlier findings.[21] Inheritance plays a key part in the continuity of farm operations, and it has been an important predictor of remaining in reasonably good financial condition in the past few years. The selectivity of the crisis, the importance of continuity through inheritance, and what turned out to be the resilience of many who "recycled" and stayed in farming despite predictions to the contrary—all have ensured that what at first seemed to be a catastrophe was not the major transformation many feared. Evidence from the sample families and from the general farm population of the state bears out the view that farming goes on much as it did before the crisis.

Farm advocates, who had a stake in the continued poor performance of the economy, were correct in stating that the downturn was far from over in 1987. But they were less accurate about the facts when they cited the increases in foreclosures by the Farm Credit System and the Farmers' Home Administration and the resulting bankruptcies as indicators that the crisis was getting worse, not better.[22]

A sample of farm bankruptcies filed in the northern district of Iowa from January to early May 1987 demonstrated that, like the farm crisis itself, bankruptcy as a means of farm reorganization had also changed. As Table 20 shows, the new Chapter 12 category, instituted the previous December, had largely taken over the role of Chapter 11. Those who filed farm bankruptcy at this juncture in the Iowa farm crisis were not new failures; these petitioners had lived in limbo for months, if not years, before they actually filed. Those with FmHA loans (47 percent of the total sample and the largest group of borrowers) had remained immune from foreclosure because of a judge's ruling two years previously. Similarly federal Land Bank borrowers had benefited from a foreclosure moratorium in place since 1985. In addition, as the debt-to-asset ratios of these cases indicate, most

Table 20. Farm Bankruptcies, Northern District, January-May
1987

Chapter 12; N = 68;	
Average debt	$629,311
Average assets	$310,534
Debt-to-asset ratio	216%
Farmers' Home Administration borrowers	37% (25)
Land Bank borrowers	41% (28)
Commercial bank borrowers	22% (15)
Chapter 7; N = 128,	
Average debt	$305,529
Average assets	$139,477
Debt-to-asset ratio	235%
Farmers' Home Administration borrowers	56% (72)
Land Bank borrowers	16% (21)
Commercial bank borrowers	27% (35)

Source: Case Records, Northern District of Iowa Bankruptcy Court, Cedar Rapids.
Note: There were 5 farm Chapter 11 cases in this period.

were in a hopeless financial position. The Chapter 12 debts were lower than those of the Chapter 11s analyzed previously, but this decline was mainly a result of the inexorable loss in the value of assets over the period of the farm crisis. In short, those who filed in early 1987 had been in irretrievable position for months. Indeed, these cases were not a good test of the effectiveness of the Chapter 12 as an instrument for reorganization of the farm business because of the hopeless financial status of the petitioners.[23]

In essence, then, these statistics were an indicator not of how bad the farm crisis was in the early months of 1987 but of the great time lag between failure and resolution. Several years before, borrowers had taken advantage of the liberal loan policy for expansion or for disaster loans, and only in 1987 was the penalty finally being paid.

One other piece of evidence not shown in the table supports this view. In many cases, particularly Chapter 7s, petitioners and their wives were no longer farming; they had held off-farm jobs for several years. As for the Chapter 12s, with debt ratios of well over 100 percent, all were instituted as holding actions to stay on the farm by attempting to force lenders to the negotiating table.

Further evidence from statewide sources indicated that economic stress was diminishing, although segments of the farm population still had chronic problems. In a study that surveyed five thousand farms in the state 50 percent of respondents were in a "strong financial position," 24 percent were "stable," and 26 percent were "weak and under severe stress." Overall, farm income had improved by an average of $16,300 from 1985 to 1986. On the other hand there was a wide variability in net income. Those in a strong financial position averaged $25,800 in net farm income, but the severely distressed group had a loss of $1,000. In addition, the farmers under pressure held roughly 50 percent of the farm debt in the state.[24]

The state-run hotline continued to receive a high volume of calls, but in 1987 most dealt with legal and emotional problems. In previous years financial queries had dominated counselors' logs. Now callers often spoke of family problems—conflict between spouses or between parents and children—an indicator that in some families the long-drawn-out struggle to save the farm had reached a crisis point.[25]

This evidence from the general Iowa farm population merits the conclusion that for the immediate future farmers will be divided into two tiers: those relatively free of financial problems and those still under severe pressure.

Without financial data it is impossible to say whether my sample families conformed to the pattern. Asked whether they intended to expand their operations in the immediate future, only 21 percent said yes; none of these farms had been hurt by the downturn. More important from the viewpoint of intergenerational operations was their feeling about whether they could continue farming until their children took over. Half said that they were certain to keep the farm in the family for another generation. Some already had children who were well established, and others were secure and saw no impediments to their achieving such a transition. A smaller number (37 percent) were less sure about their intentions, and the remainder had given up all hope of seeing another generation farm.

To be more specific what was the prognosis for the three status groups in the sample population? The evidence suggests that the majority of families have already been answered for. The yeoman familial tradition is ideally suited to corn-belt agriculture, as the farm crisis reemphasized. Conservatism and cautious, well-measured expansion would permit modest increases in size. Some, thanks to a cushion of self-financing, could grow larger. The phenomenon of recycling should benefit those prominent farmers who, though severely wounded, managed to tread water long enough to allow the economy to right itself. Adversity honed their management skills and made some quite innovative in securing financing, so that a loss of support from conventional lenders would not prevent a reentry into agriculture. For those in the select group not touched by the downturn, business contacts and accumulated resources would permit them to grow without hindrance. Ironically, one of the major obstacles to intergenerational continuity was the unwillingness of the younger generation to stay on the farm.

The group with the least opportunity to recycle careers were those from tenant backgrounds. In some instances, their intergenerational continuity had already terminated when children left to work elsewhere. For them, the seventies turned into a cruel hoax. The economic boom seemed tailor-made for bringing children into farming. But to do so, such families had to go deeply into debt. From the perspective of 1987 they, like their parents before them, could see that farming was a one-generation business, in the sense that each generation had to make it on its own. When they had started out, it was still possible to enter agriculture without much assistance. When their children began, this was no longer so. Under normal circumstances their children probably would not have thought of farming as a possible occupation, but the boom pulled them into agriculture.

Ironically the 60 percent decline in land values since 1981 was something of an advantage for those intergenerational farm families fortunate enough to emerge unscathed. The huge loss in equity solved the acute problems with estate planning and inheritance mechanisms. Not only did changes in estate tax law place exemptions at higher levels, but the decreased land values removed the need for elaborate strategies to avoid steep tax penalties for heirs. In this respect the farm crisis benefited families that had a long-term commitment to farming.

But what of the inner workings of the intergenerational farm family? What did the downturn do to the day-to-day organization of the farm and relations between and within generations? Considering that 22 percent of all farms in the sample were three-generation operations, and 46 percent had an elderly family member (aged sixty-five or over) who still had an economic interest in the operation itself, it is somewhat surprising that only 8 percent gave direct economic support to elderly relatives. For the most part, elderly family members remained independent of the family on the farm. They usually owned their own home, and while relying on income from land, often had liquid assets in the form of bank deposits as well. The evidence suggests that the elderly came through the farm crisis better than other family members. Certainly those who needed nursing care were a burden on their families, and some were shocked by the loss in equity of their land, but generally elderly ex-farmers and their spouses enjoyed a satisfying retirement. It should be remembered, after all, that for those who had gone through the Depression, austerity was something easily endured.

For the wife on the larger farm the downturn was sometimes a time of transition. In the 1970s many farm women had come to play a bigger role in the operation. Property and tax laws were updated to reflect that they usually had joint tenancy of the land with their husbands. Glossy farm magazines stressed the increasing tendency for wives to play a part in management and in the field. The boom saw the high tide of the husband-wife partnership, when the wife had a full-time role in the operation.[26] The farm crisis and changes in the aspirations of wives altered this pattern to some extent. Nevertheless, in 66 percent of all sample families no women were working off the farm; so the trend to off-farm jobs was still gathering momentum.

In some families wives were far more active and outspoken than their husbands in trying to save their farms and their livelihood. Unfortunately, many started protesting only after the farm was already in trouble. For although women were becoming less dependent and many couples made more effort to discuss management decisions on an equal basis, there remained a tendency for husbands to be less than candid when confronted with the really tough decisions. One farmer admitted that he made none of his reorganization plans known to his wife. As long as she was able to live at a standard to which she was accustomed, it was best she remain ignorant.

In general those wives untouched by the downturn "hunkered down" and returned, if they had ever left it, to what one farmer called "the nonconsumptive life," so much stressed in their mothers' generation. They soldiered on much as before with housework, child rearing, trips to town, bookkeeping, occasional field and barn work, and club and church activities. The most common response to a threat from outside was for a wife to search for off-farm work in the local community or farther afield. Women in the sample commuted long distances and worked for minimum wages to bolster the family budget. In their families considerable reorganization of the daily routine of child care and home management was necessary. Given the relatively low economic return and, in some cases, the lack of satisfaction with these jobs, it would be worth speculating if this trend would continue when the farm economy fully recovered. For a number of reasons it would seem premature to say that the farm family has lost its womenfolk permanently to off-farm employment.

As in any two-generation business, the younger is usually at some disadvantage because of a lack of autonomy. In the seventies, however, some parents could not be accused of holding their children back, for so many farms got into trouble in an attempt to bring younger members into farming. It would seem that the older generation might react to trouble by tightening the reins, by increased reluctance to surrender long-term management decisions to the younger generation. Nervous parents might prolong the time of apprenticeship on the intergenerational family farm and thwart the aspirations of the ambitious. Conversely, the existence of what might be termed "backdoor" opportunities in the rental of land could allow young farmers to begin farming on their own. The need for investors to engage reliable local tenants and their willingness to provide financing would create opportunities. For younger family members, the lowering of rents, the return to crop sharing, the availability of secondhand machinery—all results of the crisis—made tenure more open than it had been ten years before; for the lucky ones, the farm crisis gave them a start.

In sum, despite setbacks, the intergenerational family farm remained an important institution in the open-country corn belt.

Over the period of a decade Iowa farm families experienced what amounted to a shake-out in land tenure, the reorganization of farm finance, and in some cases a search for alternative sources of income. At the same time, many small farm service communities continued their accelerated decline. Family members looked beyond the home for jobs, and children who might have farmed ten years before sometimes abandoned these plans. In the space of four or five years the pendulum swung in the opposite direction. In 1982 lenders still judged farmers who wanted to borrow money by the potential value of their assets in an inflationary economy. But by 1986 some farmers who resented the treatment they had received from the banks had rejected any contact with lenders and were farming out of their back pockets with cash. Five years earlier spiraling land values had made landownership a sine qua non; in 1987 renting had returned as an acceptable way of making a living and a possible avenue of reentering agriculture for those who had failed. The downturn had shaken the faith of many farmers in the standard practices of production agriculture—the utilization of big machinery, the unrestricted use of chemicals, and the emphasis on grain monoculture—and had forced a reappraisal. There was a renewed interest in a more diversified agriculture. And with less money to pay for the expensive inputs farmers had insisted on using in their field preparation, the stalled movement to reduce chemical dependence in farming and to clean up groundwater gained momentum. Looking beyond all the broken lives and shattered communities, therefore, there were a few positive results.

In 1981 American and Iowa agriculture was about to explode. That the explosion came through savage deflation, which destroyed the plans of many who had counted on leveraged land values to make them wealthy, was unfortunate, but it forced everyone involved to reconsider how farming would be conducted in the future. If the evidence in this study has validity, it seems plain that farm families have already returned to earlier well-tried patterns. Whether the grip of agribusiness and agrifinance on family farming will be loosened remains to be seen. What is clear is that lenders, the Cooperative Extension Service, and farm suppliers and manufacturers experienced as great a trauma in the farm downturn as their clients. Presumably the lessons they learned between 1983 and 1987 will have their effects. Moreover, because of the shocks absorbed by the corporate agribusiness segment of agriculture, it would seem unlikely, despite dire predictions, that a take-over of corn-belt farming would come from this quarter.

Thus despite rapid change, the concept of the family farm remained a potent force during the farm crisis. Nonetheless, this book has to end on a cautionary note. Just as there seemed to be clear signs of economic recovery, nature intervened to make 1988 one of the driest years on record not only in Iowa but in the rest of the cornbelt. Media coverage of the drought provided urban America with graphic scenes of parched fields and livestock suffering in the high humidity and heat. But again many of the ironies of the situation were overlooked. For the crop failure, coming as it did after two years of bountiful harvests, reduced surpluses accumulated over the previous 24 months. The hot, dry conditions dramatically pushed back grain prices to levels unheard of two years before. This had the effect of eliminating the need for farm program deficiency payments.

The impact of major crop failure should not be underestimated; its consequences for farm families, agribusiness, and the consuming public are as yet unclear. But it is worth noting that the power of the agricultural lobby was clearly demonstrated once more when, in an election year, farm program provisions were redrawn to take into account the large losses that farmers were expected to incur. Whether the drought of 1988 signaled the beginning of act two of the farm crisis, as some have predicted, is impossible to say.[27]

Certainly crop losses cannot assist the recovery of those families desperately trying to pay off past debts. At the same time the argument presented here underlines the basic resilience of the cornbelt farm family to withstand even the most brutal recession brought on first by an economic downturn and then by the weather.

Appendix A
Data Collection

Sources

My research used five principal data sources during a two-year course: the press (national, statewide, local, and farm); government reports, such as those of the Extension Service; records from county courthouses and the federal bankruptcy court; a survey administered to the farm families that took part in the study; and participant observation both of the families in the study and of events and institutions in Iowa from the early spring of 1985 to the early summer of 1987.

The press was a continuous source of material and important for understanding the boom period of the seventies. The Des Moines *Register* was a vital organ of information on national and state issues as they affected farming. The paper's thorough coverage of the economic and social issues, especially the farm program, made the *Register* indispensible for following a complex situation as it evolved. The Iowa Poll, published by the paper, periodically devoted itself entirely to farm families. The farm press was far less useful. Its organs, dedicated as they were to boosting production agriculture, routinely put the best possible face on a grim situation in 1984-1985. Often it was impossible to tell from reading these magazines that anything had occurred, except for the fact that fewer advertisements were published. Once the economic corner was turned in 1986, farm magazines with a few exceptions made little effort to reflect on recent events; they preferred to plunge forward in their promotion of business as usual. The agricultural lender press was better. In an industry hard hit by farm debt, editors made an effort to publish factual and objective articles on the farm credit situation. Finally, there was a fine tradition at the Iowa Experiment Station for in-depth reports before the 1970s, but these were abandoned both because of cost and because agricultural economics is so econometrically oriented. Economists, it seems, no longer do fieldwork and are not prepared to get their boots dirty. The Cooperative Extension Service continued its polling and survey work, however, providing data that permitted an accurate reading of trends throughout the seventies and eighties.

The importance of county archival material cannot be exaggerated. Unfortunately computerization and microfilming has tended to make research more restricted in probate, the civil court, and land records. In many small rural courthouses, however, the old system of docket storage still prevails, and I had unrestricted access to deeds, mortgages, civil cases, and probate without great difficulty. During earlier research in Iowa and California, I was alerted to the value of the resources of absract and title companies. Their services allow a researcher to markedly increase the pace of data collection in company tract books.

The federal bankruptcy court maintains two districts in Iowa, one in Des Moines and the other in Cedar Rapids. During the farm crisis both courts did a brisk business, and neither was a particularly easy place to work. Bankruptcy records provide a large amount of economic data on each case. All debts are listed, with lenders' and creditors' names; assets are broken down into landed property, movable property (machinery, household goods), and income (often Internal Revenue Service tax returns are included); family occupations are noted; names and ages of family members are given; there are economic reports if the case is a Chapter 11, information from case hearings, and on occasion a synopsis of a farmer's career in farming and his intentions—whether he wants to continue in agriculture after reorganization. In short, bankruptcy data give an unusually comprehensive record of a financially distressed farm family.

The third major body of material used in the study was the survey (Appendix B). Its major objective was to collect basic demographic information and a chronological record for each intergenerational farm operation over the period 1975 to 1986. At a time when hard economic data such as income and debt ratios were difficult to calculate because of the huge losses incurred by some families (some might have resented outsider requests for this kind of information, as well), financial condition was measured by a categorical question. Questions designed to gauge opinions about ideology, the future of the family farm and community, career change, and the farm program were included to obtain a better understanding of each family's situation and attitudes. In practice the questionnaire proved reasonably functional. A number of questions dealing with reorganization were bypassed when families without problems were interviewed. In addition, there was ample opportunity to pursue points brought up in the open-ended part of the questionnaire. Under field conditions, however, I found that the elaborate scoring designations worked out for a number of answers proved impractical.

As the coding scheme shows (Appendix C), I substituted a system of dichotomous variables designed to show agreement or disagreement. These proved less time-consuming to collect, and easier to analyze on the computer.

Inasmuch as this study attempted to come to terms with all aspects of the farm family milieu, participant observation was not restricted to the interview period, or to just before or after it. Instead, I made every effort to attend activist meetings and workshops, media events, farm sales, church services, family picnics, and to take part in sporting events such as golf outings with farmers and ten-kilometer runs in the small communities where the study took place. I also attended my precinct caucus on primary day in 1986 and acted as a poll watcher at the general election.

The period before the interview and after it gave some opportunity to observe how an individual family lived and interacted. When, on occasion, participant observation and interaction involved a work situation on a farm or a more extended period of time with a family, I wrote my notes up after the visit was completed.

Sample Selection

There was a relationship between the evolution of the farm crisis and the selection and composition of the sample. Not only was the target population a specific group within the larger population (two-generation operations), but it was important to include families that had gone through or were going through reorganization, as well as those who were comparatively free of financial problems. I abandoned the idea of drawing a random sample of farm operations in each sample area when I discovered that access to the Agricultural Stabilization and Conservation records was impossible. Instead, I used what could be termed a multistage convenience sample. In Fayette County I first selected families in the summer of 1985. I sat down with a knowledgeable retired farmer and went through the county plat book, noting down the names of every two-generation farm family in the county. I then went to the courthouse and abstract company to cull as much economic and demographic information about them as possible. Courthouse work was important for two reasons. First, it allowed me to select my sample by locality, size of operation, and length of time in the neighborhood—the main selection criteria. Second, it gave me a chance to learn something about the families I was about to interview. This knowledge often gave instant rapport with the family and helped assure a warm reception.

Work did not begin in the other sample areas (Benton, Sac, and Ida

Table A.1. Comparison of the Sample Population and the
General Farm Population in Iowa

	Sample	Iowa
Age of family head	62	53
Mean acres owned	511	233
Median acres owned	350	—
Mean acres rented	412	209
Median acres rented	210	—
Raise grain exclusively	10%	33%
Making a comfortable living, December 1986	45%	40%*
Under some pressure	55%	56%

Source: Sample Data; Des Moines Sunday Register, Dec. 8 1986.
*Four percent would not give financial condition.

counties) until the summer of 1986. By then it was possible to make
much better use of county and bankruptcy records to gauge economic
stress among the farm population. A perusal of the deed books in the
recorder's office revealed foreclosures by lending institutions and the
surrender of land to contract holders. The civil case dockets kept by the
county clerk provided information on suits both by lenders against
farmers and vice-versa. Since bankruptcy is under federal jurisdiction,
no official record of it was kept in the county. In order to compile a list of
farm bankruptcies, I made several visits to the bankruptcy court of the
northern district of Iowa.

The selection process for the other sample sites showed minor
variations from that of Fayette. I lived in Benton for the duration of the
study and so had easy access to and good familarity with the farm
population in all areas of the county. I could draw up a sample of
potential respondents who were in no great difficulty, and a smaller list
of those who had suffered loss, at my leisure. In Sac and Ida, the
Extension agents initially gave me a very useful orientation to their farm
population in September 1986. Later, other key informants put me in
touch with more potential interviewees. Again, however, my best tool
was to play the detective with the available information in the public
record, compiling lists of possible families and learning as much about
them from the records as from human contact (Tables A.1, A.2).

Data Collection

Table A.2. Sample Characteristics.

Age of Father		
⟨50	9.3%	(11)
50-59	38.9	(46)
60-69	24.4	(30)
70-79	17.7	(21)
80⟩	8.1	(10)*
Age of Son		
⟨30	35.5	(44)
30-39	36.2	(49)
40-49	22.9	(31)
50⟩	8.1	(11)
Number of Families Dependent on Operation		
1	28%	(38)
2	44	(59)
3	23	(31)
4	5	(7)
Acres Owned		
⟨240	33.5%	(44)
241-500	35.1	(46)
500⟩	31.2	(41)
Organization of Farm		
Sole proprietor	60%	(81)
Partnership	22	(30)
Family corporation	18	(24)

Source: Sample Data
*In 13 percent of the families the father had died by 1986.

Table A.3. Family Farm Reorganization, by Locality, 1986-1987

	Benton County		Fayette County		Sac and Ida Counties	
	Percentage	Number	Percentage	Number	Percentage	Number
No reorganization	62	28	71	30	42	20
Reorganization	38	17	29	12	58	28

Source: Sample data.

Once I was armed with this background information, the next stage was to get in touch with the farm families themselves. Table A.3 shows the economic situation of sample families from the three areas in the winter of 1986-1987. These figures are in no way representative of economic stress in these counties as a whole, but they do reflect a continuum of difficulty across northern Iowa in the farm crisis. Because of the need for specific types of families and the limited number of cases from which to draw generalizations (135), there was some overcompensation for those in difficulties. This was especially so in Sac and Ida, where the downturn was more spectacular than elsewhere. An overall ratio of 58:42 between nonstressed and stressed families was a reasonable reflection of the state as a whole at the end of 1986.

Although farmers are very approachable, their busy schedules and relatively unstructured workday make it important for a researcher to try to complete an interview as soon as possible after the respondent has agreed to take part. Long lag times invariably lead to cancellations. Telephones are also a poor resource tool when working with farm families—quite apart from the fact that the deregulation of the telephone industry had made the rural rate structure outrageous. To make an appointment it was cheaper and more efficient to drive out to the farm, meet the family, and make a pitch for their participation in the study. Invariably, in the winter months, when most of the interviewing was done, family members were willing to sit down then and there and go through the schedule. If an immediate interview was not possible, every effort was made to arrange a session that night or the following day. Few turned me down. In general, whatever their economic circumstances, families seemed to welcome the chance to discuss their lives, their operations, and family involvement.

One of the pleasanter aspects of the research was to have the opportunity to repay a family for the time spent on the interview and the meal they often insisted on serving me. In the early stages of the study there was an opportunity to work with families in the field. Under this circumstance I was able to discuss a whole variety of issues with family members and to observe their interaction with one another. Participant observation was also the best way to arrive at an analytical classification of the family. Housing, farm machinery, food (in the home and in the field) automobiles, computer use, furnishings were added to economic behavior, family history, the extended family, and attitudes to build up a picture.

On the whole, my transformation from a researcher at home in the archives to one whose satisfactory interaction with people meant the success or failure of a day's work went fairly smoothly. On occasion I found it necessary to drive once or twice around the section road to pluck up enough courage to knock on a strange door. A few interviews were painful to conduct, owing to the reluctance of the respondents to open up. In such cases, I quickly filled out the form and left as soon as possible.

In one degree or another, the research and data collection lasted from the summer of 1985 until the spring of 1987. Members of the Fayette subsample were reinterviewed in the winter of 1986-1987 after an initial visit in 1985. Where possible, families in the other localities received a follow-up visit as well.

_____ Appendix B _____
Farm Family Survey

Name
Address
Age, education of both spouses
Type of operation
Type of organization
Members of family involved

Children: occupation, education

Years Family in Neighborhood

1970s Experience

1975: Acres owned   Rented
Enterprises
Did enterprises change during these years; if so, how?
Land Purchases, Machinery, Buildings
Lender: Short, Long
Relationship with Lender: rated 0-6 (very bad–very good)

How much consultation was required with the lender before an expansion decision was made?
1 hardly any, 2 some, 3 quite a lot, 4 complete lender control

When family had to make expansion decisions what was the family's involvement in the following situations: Buy land, rent land, change enterprise, major farm purchases, home building/remodelling/major consumption purchases, routine operations, income distribution. Scored as follows:
1 head made decision himself, 2 spouses together, 3 children and parents together

Did you have any qualms about equity financing?

4 None,
3 a few,
2 some,
1 a great deal

Did you have any difficulty obtaining funds for expansion?
Scoring same as previous question

Did you change lender in the seventies and early eighties?

Looking back on this period (1975-1983), how would you describe those years from the viewpoint of the business and the family? Rated 1-6 (extremely difficult–extremely satisfying)

There were a number of factors that impinged on farm life at that time. In regard to your operation, which caused most anxiety and stress:
Continuous inflation
High interest rates
Neighborhood competition for land (rental and bought)
Difficulty in obtaining credit
Government program (PIK)
Weather problems
Individual health problems
Livestock disease
Family differences in regard to the farm operation
Scoring 0 not applicable, 1 no effect, 2 slight, 3 moderate, 4 serious, 5 very serious

Reorganization, 1984-Present

When did you get the first signs that the downturn in the farm economy would affect your business, and what did they consist of?
The neighborhood rumor mill
Lender attitude changes
Credit checks at dealers who previously operated without them
Other

When decisions had to be made about reorganization were decisions made
Entirely by the family head?
Through consultation with the spouse?
Through consultation with children and other family members?

Lender relations:

Do you have long-term financing from the Land Bank, FmHA, insurance company, private contract

Do you require operating funds on a yearly basis? If so, from what source?

As a result of the downturn did lenders begin to dictate financial policies to you?

Did these include:

Selling land, livestock, machinery

Taking an off-farm job?

What was your attitude:

Acquiesce, move to another lender, resist and seek assistance

What reasons did the lender give for the need to reorganize your operation?

Loss of equity, high debt to asset ratio, other

At this time how aware were you of the financial implications of reorganization (i.e., taxes, deficiency payments)?

1 ignorant, 2 some knowledge, 3 considerable awareness, 4 expert knowledge

During the first stages of reorganization, did you

Attend community meetings?

Help organize a farm crisis committee in the area?

Counsel other families?

Explore the possibilities of reorganization and bankruptcy with a lawyer, CPA, or farm advocate?

During this process, which members of the family were most willing to seek assistance and advice beyond the immediate family?

1 family head, 2 spouse, 3 children, 4 equal commitment, 5 other

In seeking bankruptcy, the sale of assets, the reorganization of the enterprise, mediation, etc., has there been general agreement on the course of action within the family?

4 strong agreement, 3 agreement, 2 disagreement, 1 strong disagreement

Have you found the farm crisis years a period of no distress or profoundly distrubing? Scored 1-6 (no distress–profoundly disturbing)

How have you dealt with the trying times? 1 or 0

Great commitment to management strategies

Closer family ties emphasizing discussion
Community activity
Professional help
Individual coping
Religious commitment
Anger and hostility expressed to family members and outsiders
Others

It is easy to find scapegoats for the farm crisis. How strongly do you agree or disagree with the following statements? (4 strongly agree, 3 agree, 2 disagree, 1 strongly disagree)
The Carter administration began the downturn with the grain embargo and the failure to curb inflation
The Reagan administration has shown little understanding of the real problems of agriculture
The 1985 Farm Bill was designed as a quick fix to placate farmers but, more important, to bail out agribusiness and the banks
Farmers who used the inflationary climate of the late seventies and early eighties to expand deserve their fate
Most politicians in Iowa shamelessly used the farm crisis to get themselves elected or reelected to office
At the height of the farm crisis it was said that the Farm Bureau, the Extension Service, and the bankers, were farmers' worst enemies. Is that still the case?
Lenders learned a real lesson in the farm crisis; now they act responsibly in their relations with farmers
The only way to stay in farming nowadays is to pay off debts and not borrow money
It's important that Iowa farmers scale down their activities so they can achieve a more self-sustaining agriculture
When all is said and done, farmers are their own worst enemies: they can't organize among themselves, they take advantage of the farm program while mouthing platitudes about the free market, and they show little concern for their role as stewards of the land

The Present and the Future

How would you describe the current financial condition of your operation?
4 prospering, 3 making a comfortable living, 2 under some pressure, 1 worried about quitting farming

How has the operation changed since 1983?
Acres owned, rented; livestock; machinery; scaled-down debt

How many family members are working off the farm? What are their
jobs? For how long?

Talking about the future, express agreement or disagreement on the
following (4 strongly agree, 3 agree, 2 disagree, 1 strongly disagree):
The operation will remain unchanged in the forseeable future
This is a time to expand; we expect to take advantage of the oppor-
tunities available
We are living from one year to the next courtesy of the lender
The farm program is about the only thing between us and quitting
Mandatory controls are not the answer to the problems of agriculture
today
Athough an intergenerational farm operation is an ideal organization
for a family business, the farm crisis showed that a father/son business
arrangement is untenable today
The past few years have shown that at best farming is just a one-
generation business. When we retire, we do not expect another mem-
ber of the family to take over
The farm crisis has made early retirement a dim prospect
We are too old to change jobs now even if any were available
All in all, despite the difficulties of the past few years, this family found
the farm crisis a challenging and growing experience from which we
learned a number of lessons that will be valuable in the future
The medium-sized farm worked entirely by family labor has a future in
rural America
By the turn of the century, agriculture in Iowa will be controlled entirely
by large units, often managed from a great distance
There seems little chance that our local service community will survive
the next few years
Our community will survive because this family and others like it have
always tried to use its facilities before going to larger retail and
entertainment centers

In looking ahead, which of the following will be the greatest challenge
to the family?
Persuading the lender to provide support so as to stay in business one
more year
Trying to provide some intergenerational continuity in the family business

Trying to give equal treatment to children in an estate plan
Security for elderly family members in retirement
Securing an off-farm job for head and spouse
Attempting to farm and live comfortably on a reduced scale
Figuring the best method of expansion in a period of limited growth
potential

───── Appendix C ─────
Coding Scheme

Variables, Coding, and Column Placement

(note: all dichotomous variables were coded 1 or 0)

Identification (1-3)
1. Age of father (4, 5)
2. Age of son (6, 7)
3. Type of operation: grain 1, hogs 2, dairy 3, hogs/dairy 4, cattle/hogs 5, cattle 6 (8)
4. Organization of Operation: sole proprietor 1, partnership 2, corporation 3 (9)
5. Number of families, farm supports (10)
6. Education of father: grade school 1, high school 2, some college 3, college graduate 4 (11)
7. Education of son (as in number 6) (12)
8. Years in neighborhood: 1 a hundred years, 2 since 1930s, 3 since World War II (13)
9. Acres owned 1975 (14-17)
10. Acres rented 1975 (18-21)
11. Bought land: yes 1 no 0 (22)
12. Buildings (23)
13. Expanded enterprise (24)
14. Home remodeling (25)
15. Lender (long term): 1 land bank, 2 contract, 3 insurance, 4 commercial bank, 5 FmHA, 6 renting (26)
16. Lender (short term): 1 PCA, 2 local bank, 3 metropolitan bank, 4 self-financed, 5 FmHA (27)
17. Family decision making: 1 head only, 2 joint spouse, 3 children as well, 4 children only (28)
18. Family style: 1 conservative, 2 middle of the road, 3 professional, 4 plunger (29)
19. Family differences: 0 none, 1 intragenerational, 2 intergenerational, 3 divorce (30)

20. Assistance to children (31)
21. Heavy use of government feed grain program (32)
22. Trouble or not (33)
23. Reorganization behavior: 1 bankruptcy, 2 give back, 3 renegotiation with lender, 4 foreclosure, 5 civil litigation (34)
24. Timing: before 1985 1, 1985 2, 1986 3, 1987 4 (35)
25. Changed lender (36)
26. Sold or gave back land (37)
27. Eliminated enterprise (38)
28. Sold machinery (39)
29. Took off-farm job (40)
30. Attended community meetings (41)
31. Local activist (42)
32. Counseled friends (43)
33. Cooperative attitude with lender if in trouble (44)
34. Individual coping (45)
35. Religious faith (46)
36. Sympathy for those in difficulties (47)
37. Financial condition: 4 prospering, 3 making a comfortable living, 2 under some pressure, 1 worried about quitting farming (48)
38. Off-farm jobs: 1 service, 2 labor, 3 professional (49)
39. Expansion soon (50)
40. Will this continue as intergenerational business: 1 yes, 0 no, 2 uncertain (51)
41. Are family elderly financially secure? 1 yes, 0 no (52)
42. Close intergenerational living (53)
43. County: 1 Benton, 2 Fayette, 3 Ida/Sac (54)
44. Three-generation family (55)
45. Women job (56)
46. Catholic (57)
47. Family inherited real estate or other wealth (58)
48. Farming style: independent 0, integrated 1 (59)
49. Lawyer: none 0, local 1, metropolitan 2 (60)
50. Time in limbo: >six months 1, 1 year 2, 2 years< 3 (61)

Notes

Preface

1. Mark Friedberger, *Farm Families and Change in Twentieth Century America* (Lexington: Univ. Press of Kentucky, 1988).

2. For a general introduction to the farm crisis at the national as well as the Iowa state level, see ibid., 6-10, 190–96; and Steve H. Murdock, and F. Larry Leistritz, *The Farm Financial Crisis: Socioeconomic Dimensions and Implications for Producers and Rural Areas* (Boulder, Co., Westview Press, 1988). For the background of the Iowa farm crisis, and the ethical issues it brought to rural America, see Gary Comstock, ed., *Is There a Moral Obligation to Save the Family Farm?* (Ames: Iowa State Univ. Press, 1987), esp. 98-128; and Gordon Bultena et al., "Implications of Farm Change for a Farm State," in Joint Economic Committee of the U.S. Congress, *New Dimensions in Rural Policy: Building upon our Heritage* (Washington D.C.: Government Printing Office, 1986), 288-97; for grass roots farm family reaction see Jim Schwab, *Raising Less Corn and More Hell: Midwestern Farmers Speak Out* (Urbana: University of Illinois Press, 1988).

3. See for example, *Family Relations* 36 (1987), in which several articles are devoted to coping with farm family stress; and for the farm crisis as a whole, Neil E. Harl, "Lessons Learned from the Farm Debt Crisis of the 1980s," W.I. Myers Memorial Lecture, Dept. of Ag. Economics, Cornell University, A.E. Research 88-13, October, 1988.

Introduction: Iowa's Rural Heritage

1. Ruth Suckow, "Iowa," *American Mercury* (Sept. 1926): 39. Over fifty years later another Iowan provided a very different view with his eloquent celebration of America's prairies, of which Iowa was a major part. See John Madson, *Where the Sky Began: Land of the Tallgrass Prairie* (Boston: Houghton Mifflin, 1982).

2. Hugh Winebrenner, *The Iowa Precinct Caucuses: The Making of a Media Event* (Ames: Iowa State Univ. Press, 1987). The 1988 caucuses brought the world press to Iowa, and Iowans were given favorable reviews for the seriousness with which they took their task of choosing presidential candidates. According to one national publication, while Iowans might "look like Bartles and Jaymes," they "sound like McNeil/Lehrer," *Newsweek*, Feb. 1, 1988.

3. Richard J. Jensen and Mark Friedberger, *Education and Social Structure: An Historical Study of Iowa* (Chicago: Newberry Library, 1976).

4. See H. Roger Grant and L. Edward Purcell, eds., *Years of Struggle: The Farm Diary of Elmer G. Powers, 1931-36* (Ames: Iowa State Univ. Press, 1976).

5. Barry Bluestone and Bennett Harrison, *The Deindustrialization of America: Plant Closings, Community Abandonment, and the Dismantling of Basic Industry* (New York: Basic Books, 1982); for the impact of the recession on heartland industry and agriculture in the early 1980s, see William Greider *Secrets of the Temple: How the Federal Reserve Runs the Country* (New York: Simon and Schuster, 1987), 450-94.

6. The Farm Credit System is agriculture's major lender. In the seventies it was made up of the Federal Land Banks, which dispensed long- term loans, the Production Credit Associations, for short-term operating funds, and the Bank for Cooperatives, which lent money to farm-owned cooperatives. Because of the farm crisis, the system suffered major losses in the eighties, which resulted in a congressional bailout and a drastic reorganization. For details of the reorganization see Des Moines *Sunday Register*, Jan. 10, 1988.

7. Thomas A. Lyson, "Who Cares about the Farmer? Apathy and the Current Farm Crisis," *Rural Sociology* 51 (1986): 499.

8. Quoted in Des Moines *Register*, Oct. 24, 1982.

9. William Schneider, "Opinion Outlook," *National Journal*, Dec. 21, 1985, 2930.

10. Friedberger, *Farm Families and Change*, 199.

11. Richard A. Conner and Jeffrey P. Davidson, *Marketing Your Consulting and Professional Services* (New York: John Wiley and Sons, 1985), 3-7.

12. Tom Harkin, "The Save the Family Farm Act," in Gary Comstock ed., *Is There a Moral Obligation*, 388-96. The term *neopopulist* is used here to define the progressive elements in Iowa farm activism. See below for more discussion on their philosophy and actions.

13. See, for example, *Farmer*, Feb. 7, 1987, 8-9.

14. This unwillingness to accept help was especially evident in the early part of the farm crisis before mobilization. A study done in Missouri of farm families who left farming between 1980 and Jan. 1, 1985, found respondents extremely isolated. One farmer expressed himself thus: "People around here just stood by waiting to see if we would starve to death, and we almost did." According to the researchers this attitude was somewhat alarming in view of the county programs for "food stamps, commodity foods, physical and mental health assistance at little or no cost, access to job retraining, and other services." See William D. Heffernan and Judith Bortner Heffernan, "Testimony to the House Agriculture Subcommittee on Conservation, Credit, and Rural Development," *Rural Sociologist* 7 (1987): 525-26.

15. For more on data collection, see Mark Friedberger, "Probate and Land Records in Rural Areas," *Agricultural History* 58 (1984): 123-26.

16. Don A. Dillman, *Mail and Telephone Surveys: The Total Design Method* (New York: John Wiley and Sons, 1978).

17. For a discussion of the comparative merits of ethnographic and a more

statistically rigorous mode of research, see Susan Carol Rogers, "Mixing Para-
digms on Mixed Farming: Anthropological and Economic Views of Specialization in Illinois Agriculture," in *Farm Work and Fieldwork*, ed. Michael Chibnik
(Ithaca, N.Y.: Cornell University Press, 1987), 58-89.

18. In the sample 57 percent of all families had at least two generations
working on the farm at the time of the interview. The remainder, however, all had
intergenerational components. For example, an elderly family member who had
an interest in landownership but no management responsibility. In all 13 percent
of these families had fathers who had died before the interview took place, but
had taken part in management in the seventies.

1. Structure

1. Jack Doyle, *Altered Harvest* (New York: Viking, 1985), 29-30; John M.
Conner et al., *The Food Manufacturing Industries: Structure, Strategies, Performance and Policies* (Lexington, Mass.: Lexington Books, 1985), 163-65; Larry W.
Waterfield, *Conflict and Crisis in Rural America* (New York, Praeger, 1986),
56-59.

2. Carlisle Ford Runge, "Technological and Financial Adjustment in
American Agriculture: Who Will Quit and Why?" in *Public Policy and Agri-
cultural Technology*, ed. Don Hadwiger and William P. Browne (New York: St.
Martins Press, 1987), 33-51.

3. Marty Strange, "The Economic Structure of a Self Sustainable Agriculture," in *Meeting the Expectations of the Land: Essays in Sustainable Agriculture* ed. Wes Jackson et al. (San Francisco: North Point Press, 1985), 116-20.

4. Deborah Fink, *Open Country Iowa: Rural Women, Tradition and
Change* (Albany: State Univ. of New York Press, 1986), 59-60.

5. The classic empirical study of changes in family farming in the upper
Midwest after World War II is Peter Dorner, *Economic and Social Changes on
Wisconsin Family Farms (A Sample of Wisconsin Farms—1950, 1960, 1975)*
(Madison: College of Agricultural and Life Sciences, Univ. of Wisconsin, R3105,
Feb. 1981). For Iowa, see Friedberger, *Farm Families and Change*, 20-22.

6. David B. Danbom, *The Resisted Revolution: Urban America and the
Industrialization of Agriculture* (Ames: Iowa State Univ. Pres, 1979).

7. George M. Beal, *The Adoption of Two Farm Practices in a Central Iowa
County*, Iowa Agricultural Experiment Station, Special Report 26 (1960): 7-12.

8. William L. Flinn and Frederick H. Buttel, *Sociological Consequencs of
Farm Size: The Family Farm and Ideological and Social Consequences of Scale
in Agriculture*, Cornell Rural Sociology Bulletin 114 (1980): 28-29.

9. Philip Raup, *Family Farming: Rhetoric and Reality*, Miscellaneous Journal Series, Minnesota Agricultural Experiment Station Paper 2147 (1986): 6.

10. John W. Bennett, *Of Time and the Enterprise* (Minneapolis: Univ. of
Minnesota Press, 1982); Seena B. Kohl, *Working Together: Women and Family in
Southwestern Saskatchewan* (Toronto: Holt, Rinehart and Winston, 1976).

11. Sonya Salamon and Kathleeen Markan, "Incorporation and the Farm Family," *Journal of Marriage and the Family* 46 (1984): 167- 78.

12. Quoted in Des Moines *Sunday Register*, April 8, 1979.

13. L. Bharaswaj and E.A. Wilkening, "Occupational Satisfaction of Farm Husbands and Wives," *Human Relations* 27 (1974): 739; Janet Bokemeier and Lorraine Garkovich, "Assessing the Influence of Farm Women's Self-Identity on Task Allocation and Decision Making," *Rural Sociology* 51 (1987): 13-36.

14. Mark Friedberger, "The Farm Family and the Inheritance Process: Evidence from the Cornbelt, 1870-1950," *Agricultural History* 57 (1983): 1-13; Mark Friedberger, "Handing Down the Home Place: Farm Inheritance Strategies in Iowa, 1870-1945," *Annals of Iowa* 47 (1984): 518-36.

15. Paul C. Rosenblatt and Roxanne Anderson, "Interaction in Farm Families: Tension and Stress," in *The Family in Rural Society*, ed. R.T. Coward and M.W. Smith (Boulder, Colo.: Westview Press, 1981), 147-66; Paul C. Rosenblatt and L.O. Keller, "Economic Vulnerability and Economic Stress in Farm Couples," *Family Relations* 32 (1983): 567-73.

16. Friedberger, *Farm Families and Change*, 90-97; Paul C. Rosenblatt and Roxanne Anderson, "Family Conflict over Inheritance of Property," *Family Coordinator* 28 (1979): 337-46.

17. One sample family was paying out a quarter of a million dollars in estate taxes as a result of the death of a parent just before the change in the law. Their difficulties in 1986 were partly caused by the need to make these stiff payments.

18. Candyce Russell et al., "Coping Strategies Associated with Intergenerational Transfer of the Family Farm," *Rural Sociology* 50 (1985): 361-76.

19. Randy R. Weigel, Daniel J. Weigel, and Joan Blundall, "Stress, Coping, and Satisfaction: Generational Differences in Farm Families," *Family Relations* 36 (1987): 45-48.

20. Sonya Salamon and Vicki Lockhart, "Land Ownership and the Position of Elderly in Farm Families," *Human Organization* 39 (1980): 324-30.

21. Philip Raup, *What Prospective Changes May Mean for Agriculture and Rural America in Farm Policy: The Emerging Agenda*, Missouri Agricultural Experiment Station, Special Report 338 (1985): 38.

22. Friedberger, *Farm Families and Change*, 121-25.

23. Roe C. Black, "A New Era for Agriculture," *Farm Journal* (March 1977): 21.

24. Wendell Berry, "A Defense of the Family Farm," in Comstock ed., *Is There a Moral Obligation?* 354.

25. Ian R.M. Bain and JoAnn Paulson, "Financial Stress in Agriculture: Its Causes and Extent," *Minnesota Agricultural Economist* 651, Special Issue 1 (1986): 1-12.

26. Des Moines *Register*, July 15, 1982.

27. Des Moines *Sunday Register*, Jan. 12, 1986, Feb. 15 1987. For national trends in agricultural bank failures, see *Business Week*, Sept. 30, 1985, 90-91.

28. U.S. Department of Agriculture, *A Time Choose: Summary Report on the Structure of Agriculture* (Washington, D.C.: Government Printing Office, 1981), 118, 122; William McD. Herr and Eddy La Due, "The Farmers' Home

Administration's Changing Role and Mission," *Agricultural Finance Review* 41 (1981): 58-72.

29. Des Moines *Sunday Register*, Sept. 14, 28, 1986.

30. Eric O. Hoiberg and Wallace Huffman, *Profile of Iowa Farms and Farm Families, 1976*, Iowa Agricultural Experiment Station Bulletin P141 (1978): 13; national trends can be found in Paul D. Warner and James A. Christensen, *The Cooperative Extension Service: A National Assessment* (Boulder, Col., Westview, 1984), p. 61.

31. Des Moines *Register*, April 10, 1979.

32. Bruce Marion, *The Organization and Performance of the U.S. Food System* (Lexington, Mass.: Lexington Books, 1986).

33. Roger Burbach and Patricia Flynn, *Agribusiness and the Americas* (New York: Monthly Review Press, 1980), 221-52.

34. Quoted in Des Moines *Sunday Register*, April 6, 1986; for commodity groups' participation in the writing of the 1985 Farm Bill, see William P. Browne, *Private Interests, Public Policy, and American Agriculture* (Lawrence: Univ. Press of Kansas, 1988), 233-34.

35. Fresno *Bee*, May 24, 1987.

36. Des Moines *Sunday Register*, Jan. 25, 1987.

37. National Commission on Food Marketing, *Organization and Competition in the Livestock and Meat Industry* (Washington, D.C.: Government Printing Office, 1966), 9.

38. IBP was founded in the 1960s with a $300,000 loan from the Small Business Administration. See Jimmy M. Skaggs, *Prime Cut: Livestock Raising and Meat Packing in the United States, 1607-1983 (College Station: Texas A&M Univ. Press, 1986) 190*; Des Moines *Sunday Register*, Jan. 25, 1987.

39. Partly as a result of union efforts and national publicity, IBP was fined a record $2.6 million by the Occupational Safety and Health Administration for violations of health and safety regulations at one of its plants in Nebraska. The evidence suggested that workers in Iowa plants labored under similar conditions. See Des Moines *Sunday Register*, July 26, Aug. 2, 1987.

40. Ibid., Oct. 12, 1986.

41. Ibid., Sept. 7, 1977.

42. Ibid., April 6, 1986.

43. Des Moines *Register*, Jan. 30, 1979.

44. Iowa Farm Bureau *Spokesman*, Sept. 25, 1985.

45. *Association Management* (Nov. 1986): 28-33.

46. Friedberger, *Farm Families and Change*, 119-20.

47. USDA, *A Time to Choose*, 92; for the implications of the 1986 tax revisions for farming, see Marty Strange, *Family Farming: A New Economic Vision* (Lincoln, Ne.: University of Nebraska Press, and Institute for Food and Development Policy, 1988), 163.

2. Boom

1. The Hartman story is taken from Calvin Trillin, "U.S. Journal: Grundy County, Iowa: A Father-Son Operation," *The New Yorker, Sept. 20, 1982, 98-109.*

2. Ironically despite Lawrence's eventual conviction, he still owned the family land. In an out-of-court settlement, the sons were given the right to farm the property while paying their father $200,000 down, and $30,000 a year for the next thirty years. Only a short time later the bubble in Iowa land values burst, leaving the sons holding expensive mortgages and with reduced resources to pay them off.

3. Des Moines *Sunday Register*, Sept. 14, 1976.

4. Ibid., Sept. 14, 1976, March 20, 1977.

5. Ibid., June 25, 1976.

6. For Land Bank and Production Credit Association expansion, see Friedberger, *Farm Families and Change*, 115-18, 121-23.

7. See Donald Johnson and Michael Boehlje, *Investment, Production, and Marketing Strategies for an Iowa Cattle Feeder in a Risky Environment*, Iowa Agricultural Experiment Station Research Bulletin 592 (1981): 85-86. After 1984, Iowa cattle feeders, like their peers in the West, increasingly sought to allay the risks of cattle feeding by doing custom work for investors. Of course, in so doing they were no longer working for themselves.

8. Odebolt *Chronicle*, June 21, 1979.

9. Rex R. Campbell, William D. Heffernan, and Jere Lee Gilles, "Farm Operator Cycles and Farm Debts: An Accident of Timing," *Rural Sociologist* 4 (1984): 404-8.

10. Willard W. Cochrane, *The Development of American Agriculture: A Historical Analysis* (Minneapolis: Univ. of Minnesota Press, 1979), 387-95.

11. Gordon Bultena, Paul Lasley, and Jack Geller, "The Farm Crisis: Patterns and Impacts of Financial Stress among Iowa Farm Families," *Rural Sociology* 51 (1986): 436-48.

12. See James Lowenberg-Deboer, *The Microeconomic Roots of the Farm Crisis* (New York: Praeger, 1986), 157.

13. Des Moines *Sunday Register*, Jan. 8, March 26 1978.

14. Des Moines *Register* and *Sunday Register*, April 8-15, 1979.

15. Des Moines *Register*, April 14, 1979; see Browne, *Private Interests, Public Policy*, 66-72, for an analysis of the failure of the American Agriculture Movement.

3. Storm over the Country

1. Ronald C. Kessler, Richard H. Price, and Camille B. Wortman, "Social Factors to Psychopathology: Stress, Social Support, and Coping Processes," *Annual Review of Psychology* 36 (1985): 531-72; William D. Heffernan and Judith Bortner Heffernan, "Impact of the Farm Crisis on Rural Families and Communities," *Rural Sociologist* 6 (1986): 166-70.

2. For insights into why support from neighbors was often not forthcoming in the farm crisis, see Sara E. Wright and Paul C. Rosenblatt, "Isolation and Farm Loss: Why Neighbors May Not Be Supportive," *Family Relations* 36 (1987), 391-95.

3. On right-wing extremism in rural America in the seventies and eighties, see James Coates, *Armed and Dangerous: The Rise of the Survival Right* (New York: Hill and Wang, 1987), 104-122.

4. In New York very similar patterns emerged. There, farm families faced four major problems: they lacked knowledge about the basics of reorganization (bankruptcy, foreclosure, tax implications); they could not obtain qualified legal counsel; they had difficulty getting off-farm jobs; and they suffered a crisis of identity and found making a new start a trial. See Kate Graham and John Brake, "Losing the Family Farm," *New York Food and Life Science Quarterly* 20 (1987): 9-10.

5. Statewide and county figures for 1980-85 were published in the Des Moines *Register*, Aug. 26, 1987.

5. Carroll *Today*, Feb. 11, 1986.

7. These differences were significant to the .01 level.

4. Mobilization

1. The background of the "new" populism (or, as it is called here, neopopulism) in rural America can be found in Harry C. Boyte et al., *Citizen Action and the New American Populism* (Philadelphia: Temple Univ. Press, 1986), 133-45, 153-61. For a critical view of neopopulism and agriculture, see Carlisle Ford Runge, "Neopopulism and the New Agriculture" (Unpublished paper, Department of Agricultural and Applied Economics, University of Minnesota, Dec. 1986).

2. Des Moines *Register*, May 4, 1987. It is important to note that the photograph was taken at the Small Business Administration, an agency with only a small farm-loan portfolio. By 1986 the Farm Credit System and the FmHA would not have allowed a photographer into a private business meeting with a borrower. In addition, it should be pointed out that according to the story accompanying the photo essay, despite all the trauma of losing the farm, the family had made a successful transition to another career. The farmer had begun driving a truck for a long-distance moving company. In effect the piece while pointing to the traumatic loss of the farm suggested that a successful career change was possible for a middle-aged farmer. More details of this family's struggles can be found in Schwab, *Raising Less Corn*, 47-51.

3. See, for example, James Krohe, Jr., "Hollywood's Myth Makers Peddle Family Hogwash," *Wall Street Journal*, May 23, 1985.

5. Interview with Hank Osterwald, Iowa Mediation Service, Sac City, Iowa, Feb. 25, 1987.

6. Jerry Perkins, "Loan Mediation Laws," *Agri Finance* (Sept. 1986): 19-22.

7. Holstein *Advance*, Jan. 3, 1985.

8. Odebolt *Chronicle*, May 2, 1985.

9. Iowa State University, *Self-Help Groups: Neighbor to Neighbor*, Iowa Cooperative Extension Service FE-F-270a (1985): 1-8.

10. Odebolt *Chronicle*, Nov. 7, 1985.

11. Judith Bortner Heffernan and William D. Heffernan, "Is the Church Open to Victims of the Rural Crises?" *Catholic Rural Life* (Sept. 1986): 8.

12. On the organization of the Catholic response through the rural life directors, see Dawn Hoffman Price, "The Church Responds through Rural Life Directors," *Catholic Rural Life* (Sept. 1986): 16.

13. Lynn M. LoPucki, "A General Theory of the Dynamics of the State Remedies/Bankruptcy System," *Wisconsin Law Review* (1982), 312.

14. Teresa A. Sullivan, et al., "Limiting Access To Bankruptcy Discharge: An Analysis of Creditors' Data," *Wisconsin Law Review*, (1983), 1096.

15. Alex McIntosh and Mary Zey-Ferrell, "Lending Officers' Decisions to Recommend Innovative Technology," *Rural Sociology* 51 (1986): 471. For an introduction to bank control theory, see Beth Mintz and Michael Schwartz, *The Power Structure of American Business* (Chicago: Univ. of Chicago Press, 1985).

16. For a general introduction to the problems of bank failure see Irvine H. Sprague, *Bailout: An Insider's Account of Bank Failures and Resources* (New York: Basic Books, 1986); see Des Moines *Sunday Register*, April 7, 1985, May 3, 1987, for statistics on the performance of every bank in the state in this period.

17. Herbert Swartz, "Lender Liability," *United States Banker* (May 1986): 10-22. On bank examinations by the FDIC, see Steve Cocheo, "Anatomy of an Examination," *ABA Banking Journal* (Feb. 1986): 33-38. For one Iowa bank's solution to working with problem loans, see Larry Henson, "Lenders of Interest," *Agri Finance* (Nov. 1986): 18.

18. James A. Lodoen, "Chapter 11 Farm Reorganization: Farmer Beware!" *Journal of Agricultural Taxation and Law* 9 (1987): 99-119.

19. The contemporary court experience of a farmer under financial stress is summarized in Nancy Blodgett, "Saving the Family Farm," *ABA Journal*, Jan. 1, 1988, 86-89.

20. For a background to the rural legal profession, see Donald D. Landon, "Clients, Colleagues, and Community: The Shaping of Zealous Advocacy in a Country Law Practice," *American Bar Foundation Research Journal* (1985), 81-111. For an insider's view of a country practice in the Nebraska farm crisis, see Patrick G. Rogers, "Diary of a Country Lawyer: Reflections on a Community in Crisis," *Compleat Lawyer* (Fall 1985): 14-15.

21. The Iowa Bar Association also had its own hotline. On attorney advocacy during the farm crisis, see James T. Massey, "Farm Bankruptcies: A Bitter Harvest," (Fall 1985): 7-8, 11-13; and John K. Pearson and Barbara J. Coen, "Bankruptcy Counseling for the Distressed Farmer," *Compleat Lawyer* (Summer 1986): 57-62. For a suggestion by a California lawyer, see A. Barry Cappello, "Expand Your Practice to Help Farmers: Attack Loan Problems," *Compleat Lawyer* (Spring 1987): 60-61.

22. Des Moines *Sunday Register*, Jan. 10, 1988; Floyd E. Stoner, "The Fight for Farmer Mac," *ABA Banking Journal* (Feb. 1988): 78, 82, 84.

5. Survival

1. Friedberger, *Farm Families and Change*, 104-06.

2. Paul C. Rosenblatt and L.O. Keller, "Economic Vulnerability and Economic Stress in Farm Couples," *Family Relations* 32 (1983): 567-73; Candyce Russell et al., "Coping Strategies Associated with Intergenerational Transfer of the Family Farm," *Rural Sociology* 50 (1985): 361-76; Rosalie Norem and Joan Blundall, "Farm Families and Marital Disruption during a Time of Crisis" (Unpublished paper kindly supplied by the authors).

3. A deficiency payment was calculated by subtracting the selling price of the forfeited parcel of land from the original amount of the note. Obviously in a deflationary land market this sum could be disastrous for a struggling farm family.

4. Coates, *Armed and Dangerous*, 104-22.

5. Des Moines *Sunday Register*, April 26, 1987.

6. Kenneth A. Root, "Help for Dislocated Farmers: Acceptable Alternatives," *Rural Development News* (April 1987: 5-7.

7. Paul C. Rosenblatt and Roxanne Anderson, "Interaction in Farm Families: Tension and Stress," in Coward and Smith, *The Family in Rural Society*, 147-66.

8. Patterns of off-farm work for women in the seventies are discussed in Rachel Ann Rosenfeld, *Farm Women: Work, Farm, and Family in the United States* (Chapel Hill: Univ. of North Carolina Press, 1985); but see the New York *Times*, Jan. 3, 1988, for entrepreneurship among southern Iowa women working in craftware for the "upscale" metropolitan market.

9. Des Moines *Register*, June 4, 1987.

6. The Frugal Farmer

1. Harold R. Capener and A.D. Berkowitz, "The Farm Family: A Unique Organization," *New York Food and Life Science Quarterly* 9 (1976): 8-11.

2. This discussion is based on a multiple classification analysis of sample farm families in which financial condition was measured dichotomously: either good or bad. The results conformed to a continuum with one end 100 (the best condition) and the other 0 (the poorest). Thus hog-dairy scored 95; hogs, 52; dairy, 42; cattle-hogs, 42; grain farms 39; and cattle feeders 31. These results were significant at the .07 level.

3. Inheritors had a financial condition score of 60 compared to a 26 for noninheritors. At the same time, expanders scored 38, while nonexpanders had 61. These results from a multiple classification analysis were statistically significant at the .01 level.

4. For a possible scenario for agriculture in the next decade see U.S. Congress, Office of Technological Assessment, *Technology, Public Policy and the Changing Structure of Agriculture* (Washington D.C.: Government Printing Office, 1986); the subject of rapid change and the elimination of family farms by large corporate farms is discussed in Mark Friedberger, *Farm Families and Change*, 246-51.

5. One unobtrusive measure of the "style" of farm families was the kind of lunch delivered to the work crew in the field. Some were quite elaborate, with

ice-cold soft drinks much in evidence. The families who consumed several cases of pop a week had a different sense of financial priorities from those who served iced tea in the field. (Those who served beer had still another set of priorities.) Perhaps styles in food and beverage consumption needed to change with economic cycles. Somehow Kool-aid and peanut butter sandwiches seemed to sit right in the farm crisis.

6. For its impact on Iowa agriculture, see Gordon Bultena, Paul Lasley, and Jack Geller, "Is There a Crisis Mentality in American Agriculture? A Look at the 'Hunkering Down' Behavior of American Farmers" (Unpublished paper kindly supplied by the authors).

7. Estate and inheritance tax regulations after World War II required family members to pay taxes on land transfered to them by relatives. Similarly, the old method of intervivos transfer, in which a piece of land was simply deeded over to a family member at no charge, was eliminated. At the same time, regulations in the new tax code allowed families to transfer land in the form of a gift through an estate plan over a comparatively long period of time. See Friedberger, *Farm Families and Change*, 78-83, 87-97.

8. Sonya Salamon, "Middle-Range Farmers Persisting through the Agricultural Crisis," *Rural Sociology* 51 (1986): 503-12.

7. Retrospect and Prospect

1. U.S. Department of Agriculture, *Economic Indicators of the Farm Sector: State Farm Summary, 1985* (Washington, D.C.: Government Printing Office, 1987), 178-81.

2. The Iowa experience was not unique. For the fragmentation of the farm lobby in the seventies and eighties left a vacuum in Washington and in other farm states. According to one observer, what he called the "universe of interest groups" was beyond manageable proportions and so little was accomplished to alter farm policy. This was especially notable while the 1985 Farm Bill was being debated. While he emphasized the chronic factionalism of the farm lobby, which he suggested tended to lessen the influence of powerful agribusiness and farm organizations on agricultural policy, such an interpretation ignores the disruptions which the farm crisis brought to the farm establishment which hampered their actions. See Browne, *Private Interests, Public Policy, and American Agriculture*, 106-108, 213-236; for Iowa farmer opinion on the 1985 Farm Bill, see Des Moines *Register*, May 16 1987.

3. Des Moines *Register*, Nov. 16, 1986.

4. Boyte, *Citizen Action and The New American Populism*, 183-84.

5. Des Moines *Register*, May 20, 1987.

6. *Neoconservatives* were those former political liberals who moved to the right during the Reagan years. Sparsely represented among the farm community itself, most neoconservatives came from the East Coast, where their observation of the federal government allowed them to take aim at such hallowed liberal

issues as the importance of the family farm for America and to influence the urban electorate, which had little knowledge of agriculture.

7. Gregg Easterbrook, "Making Sense of Agriculture," *Atlantic* (July 1985): 63-78.

8. Jeffrey L. Pasley, "the Idiocy of Rural Life," *New Republic*, Dec. 11, 1986, 26.

9. *Ibid.*, 27. Further wit and wisdom on farmers, the Farm program, and the effect of the 1988 drought can be found in TRB, "They Asked for It," *New Republic*, July 18 and 25, 1988, 42.

10. U.S. House of Representatives, *Problems of Farm Credit*, 99th Cong. (Washington, D.C.: Government Printing Office, 1986), 82.

11. Perhaps it was not surprising that such a farm family should have the latest market gadgetry, for in the Economics Department at Iowa State, where the eldest son went to school, T.V. screens with market information were prominently displayed at strategic locations in the hallways.

12. Des Moines *Sunday Register*, March 22, 1987.

13. See Des Moines *Register*, Oct. 16, 1986, for a concise explanation of PIK and ROLL.

14. California cotton and wheat ranchers became specialists in "sidestepping" farm program regulations. See Friedberger, *Farm Families and Change*, 120-21.

15. Des Moines *Register*, April 21, 1987.

16. "Absentee Farm Owners," *Agri Finance* (Dec. 1984): 32-38.

17. James M. Hagen and Philip Raup, "The Minnesota Rural Real Estate Market in 1986," *Minnesota Agricultural Economist* 653 (1987): 4-5.

18. Des Moines *Sunday Register*, May 24, 1987.

19. *Ibid.*, May 31, 1987.

20. Don E. Albrecht and John K. Thomas, "Farm Tenure: A Retest of Conventional Knowledge," *Rural Sociology* 51 (1986): 18-30.

21. Friedberger, *Farm Families and Change*, 74-98.

22. Des Moines *Register*, May 16 1987.

23. Neil E. Harl, "Analyzing Chapter 12 Bankruptcy: A Constructive Solution or a Disaster to Ag. Lending," *Agri Finance* (March 1987): 14-15; Chris Faiferlick and Neil E. Harl, "The Chapter 12 Bankruptcy Experience in Iowa," *Journal of Agricultural Taxation and Law* 9 (1988): 302-36.

24. The survey was not as reliable as it might have been, for only 709 usable returns were gathered. Iowa State University, *Iowa Farm Finance Survey*, Iowa Cooperative Extension Assist 15 (1987): 4-12.

25. Telephone interview with Fran Philips, Des Moines, Iowa, June 10, 1987.

26. See Rosenfeld, *Farm Women*: 107-109, 182, for decision making and work patterns in the seventies.

27. Rex R. Campbell, "The Farm Crisis: Only an Intermission," *Rural Sociologist* 7 (1987): 533-36, argues that the improvement in agriculture in 1986-87 was only temporary. He foresaw further trials in the form of new technology and intermittent recessions, "like storm clouds on the horizon looming ever closer."

These problems would batter farming in the not too distant future. His prediction came well before the severe drought of 1988 sent corn and soybean futures skyrocketing and reawakened fears that the storm clouds would indeed return. For the possibility of further bankruptcies, see Des Moines *Register*, Aug. 23, 1988. An explanation of the farm program drought revisions was given in the Des Moines, *Sunday Register*, Aug. 14, 1988.

Index

Index

145-51; and control of countryside, 159-60; and decline of land values, 163-64

Farm Bureau, 18, 82, 88; organization in 1970s, 39; in crisis, 112, 150

Farm Credit System, 5-6, 28, 32, 35, 85, 97, 139; policies in downturn, 68; bailout of, 87, 103; pressure on farmers, 116-17; land ownership, 157

farm crisis: mobilization in, 10, 81-103; victims of, 10, 104; committees, 72

farmer-lender confrontation, 5, 68-71, 95-102

Farmer-Rancher Congress, 86

Farmers' Grain Dealers Association, 35

Farmers' Home Administration, 16, 28, 30, 85, 97, 105, 142; expansion in 1970s, 31-32, 46, 77; and ownership of land, 157

farm failure: stigma and trauma, 63-64; who "got into trouble," 64-67; options in, 68-72; upper class behavior in, 69, 109-14; dirt farmer behavior in, 69; pro se activity in, 70, 91; and "do-nothing" syndrome, 72; surrender of assets in, 77; peer group assistance in, 93-94; period of limbo in, 104-05; and family solidarity, 105-09; and confrontation versus accommodation, 114-15; effect of sudden death on, 116-17; inheritance as factor in, 130-40; exodus brings relief in, 149

farm families: researching, 10-14; and stress, 12, 58, 75-76, 116-17, 124, 162; sample of, 114; status of, 18-19; strategies for expansion, 25-26; business relations of, 27-29; behavior in boom, 42-45; borrowing behavior in 1970s, 47-51; and expansion pressures, 51-55; operator characteristics of, 53-54; and age, 55-57; independent behavior of, 63-64; and "do nothing" syndrome,

72; surrender of assets by, 77; quitting farming, 78-79; "circuit riders," 94; solidarity of, 105-09; and off-farm work, 121-24; disruption of, 124-26; "independent" and "integrated," 127-29; and inheritance, 137; and farm programs, 151, 156

farm inputs, 20, 27

farm programs, 8-9, 151-56; payments in 1980s, 144; 1985 Farm Bill, 144-45; temptation for abuse of, 151, 154; unfairness to diversified operators, 154; red tape and regulations of, 155

farm reorganization, 70-71

farm women, 13, 25; daughters-in-law, 26; upper-class, 112-14; outspokenness of, 120-21, 164; off-farm work, 121-22, 124, 164-65

Fayette County, Iowa, 11, 14-15

Federal Deposit Insurance Corporation, 92-93, 116, 135

Federal Land Bank, 27, 30, 46, 49, 76, 100, 107-08, 111, 113, 120, 149; move to banks for lower interest rates, 51; tactics to recover assets, 115-16

Federal Reserve System, 32

financial condition: of farmers, 128, 162; of types of operation, 129

Food Security Act, 1985, 144-45. See also farm programs

food stamps, 125

foreclosures, 58, 71

frugality: of farm families, 130-33; and professionalism, 133-36

Gallup, George, 2

Grassley, Charles, 85

Great Depression, 42

Grundy County, Iowa, 42

Hartman family, 42-44

Harvestores, 38

Hawkeye Bank Corporation, 31

helping professions, 93-94

hog-dairy enterprise, 131

Holstein, Iowa, 91